I Heart Oregon (& Washington)

25 OF THE PORTLAND AREA'S BEST HIKES

by Lisa D. Holmes

D1737699

Cover and interior design by Lisa D. Holmes (Yulan Studio, yulanstudio.com)

All photographs, maps and graphics are by the author.

Overview, geology and section maps utilize terrain map data by OpenStreetMap, under CC-BY-SA.

Contributor for geology highlights: Kaitlyn Allegretti

Published in Portland, Oregon, by Yulan Studio, Inc.

Printed in the United States.

First edition

ISBN 978-0-9915382-0-1

Contents

Contents *(continued)*

WHAT'S DIFFERENT ABOUT THIS HIKING BOOK?

It's a highly visual full-color book with 400+ photos and customized maps displayed throughout. Four pages are dedicated to each hike, which include up to 15 color photos and detailed maps featuring topography, marked trails, distances, elevation, and trail highlights. As a graphic designer, I've focused on making the book's design easy to use and providing a much more visual approach to the subject than currently exists.

WHO IS THE BOOK FOR?

Anyone who loves to spend time in the outdoors. Most of the hikes covered are easy to moderate in difficulty, with only a few that are more difficult challenges. You don't need to be an avid hiker, but I hope you will become one after exploring the areas covered in this book. Along with several hikes that are well known and popular, I've shown areas that are less familiar yet still have enough interesting features to make a longer drive or extra physical effort on the trail well worth it.

WHAT AREAS DOES IT COVER?

Instead of trying to cover all hiking possibilities in the region, I focused on 25 hikes that I consider to be the best in the Portland region: ranging from the Oregon Coast to Mount Hood, and from Southwest Washington to the Willamette-Santiam region.

SAFETY NOTICE

This book is intended as a resource to help plan a hike. Although every attempt has been made to provide accurate and current information on the hikes in this book, the publisher and the author are not responsible for any loss, damage or injury that may occur as a result of using this book – you hike at your own risk. Familiarize yourself with the area you intend to explore, check current weather reports, and check with regional recreation organizations listed in the Resource section of this book for more information on current conditions. You are responsible for your own safety and knowing your own limitations.

ABOUT THE AUTHOR

I'm a graphic designer by trade and a hiking fanatic by accident. Using the Bachelor of Fine Arts degree I earned at the Kansas City Art Institute, I've spent more than 20 years designing a successful career. But my life changed when I moved to Oregon in 2007 and became obsessed with the beauty of the Pacific Northwest landscape. I've since spent much of my time hiking the trails of Oregon and Washington and taking photographs of everything I've encountered... over 8,000 photos so far. Combining my photos, my map and book design skills, and my desire to share my journey with others has led me to a new career of creating books about the landscape I love. I live and work in SE Portland with my husband, John Vincent, and our two dogs, Sadie and Cricket.

Hike Matrix

	DISTANCE	ELEV. GAIN	DRIVE TIME	BEST SEASON	HIKE DIFFICULTY	FEATURES
1 Triple Falls and beyond	6.4 miles	1,200 ft.	40 min.	April - June & Oct. - Nov.	3	waterfalls, creeks, forest
2 Eagle Creek to High Bridge	6.6 miles	600 ft.	45 min.	April - June & Oct. - Nov.	2	waterfalls, creeks, forest
3 Herman Creek Pinnacles	4.8 miles	1,020 ft.	1 hour	April - June & Oct. - Nov.	2	forest, creeks, waterfall, geologic features
4 Wahkeena/Multnomah Falls loop	5.4 miles	1,600 ft.	35 min.	April - June & Oct. - Nov.	1	waterfalls, creeks, forest
5 Hamilton Mountain	7.6 miles	2,000 ft.	1 hour	April - June	4	waterfalls, creeks, forest, views
6 Klickitat River Trail	8 miles	125 ft.	1 hour, 30 min.	April - May	1	sunny skies, river, Native American fishing
7 McNeil Point	9.6 miles	2,220 ft.	1 hour, 40 min.	Aug. - Oct.	4	forest, alpine meadows, mountain views, glaciers
8 Ramona Falls	7 miles	1,100 ft.	1 hour, 25 min.	May - June	3	waterfall, creeks, forest
9 Salmon River Canyon	7.2 miles	950 ft.	1 hour, 15 min.	May - Sept.	2	river, forest, canyon views, wildflowers
10 Twin Lakes snowshoe	4.2 miles	700 ft.	1 hour, 40 min.	Dec. - Feb.	2	snow, forest, lake
11 Tom Dick & Harry Mountain	6.4 miles	1,500 ft.	1 hour, 15 min.	June - Aug.	3	forest, lake, mountain views
12 Tamanawas Falls via Polallie Trail	4.2 miles	900 ft.	1 hour, 30 min.	June - Oct.	3	waterfall, creek, forest
13 Lost Lake Butte	4.6 miles	1,300 ft.	2 hours	July - Sept.	3	lake, mountain views, old-growth forest
14 Saddle Mountain	5.6 miles	1,700 ft.	1 hour, 30 min.	May - June	4	coastal forest, views, wildflowers
15 Cape Falcon + Short Sand Beach	5 miles	260 ft.	1 hour, 45 min.	all year	1	coastal forest, ocean views, whale watching
16 Cape Lookout	5.2 miles	450 ft.	1 hour, 45 min.	all year	2	coastal forest, ocean views, whale watching
17 Netarts Spit	10.6 miles	0 ft.	1 hour, 45 min.	all year	2	beach, ocean views, bay
18 Ecola State Park	2-3 miles	200 - 1,000 ft.	1 hour, 30 min.	all year	2	beaches, coastal forest, ocean views, whale watching
19 Falls Creek Falls	6.3 miles	1,150 ft.	1 hour, 30 min.	May - June	3	waterfall, creeks, canyon view
20 Indian Heaven Wilderness	6.8 miles	1,500 ft.	2 hours, 30 min.	Sept. - Oct.	3	fall color, alpine meadows, lakes, mountain views
21 Siouxon Creek	7.7 miles	700 ft.	1 hour, 40 min.	May - June	2	waterfalls, creeks, forest
22 June Lake	4 miles	750 ft.	1 hour, 45 min.	July - Oct.	2	mountain views, lake, geologic features
23 Trail of Ten Waterfalls	7.7 miles	700 ft.	1 hour, 40 min.	all year	2	waterfalls, creeks
24 Jefferson Park	10.4 miles	1,800 ft.	2 hours, 20 min.	Aug. - Sept.	4	forest, alpine meadows, lakes, mountain views
25 Opal Creek	7.1 miles	300 ft.	2 hours	May - June	2	mining history, waterfalls, forest, river, creeks

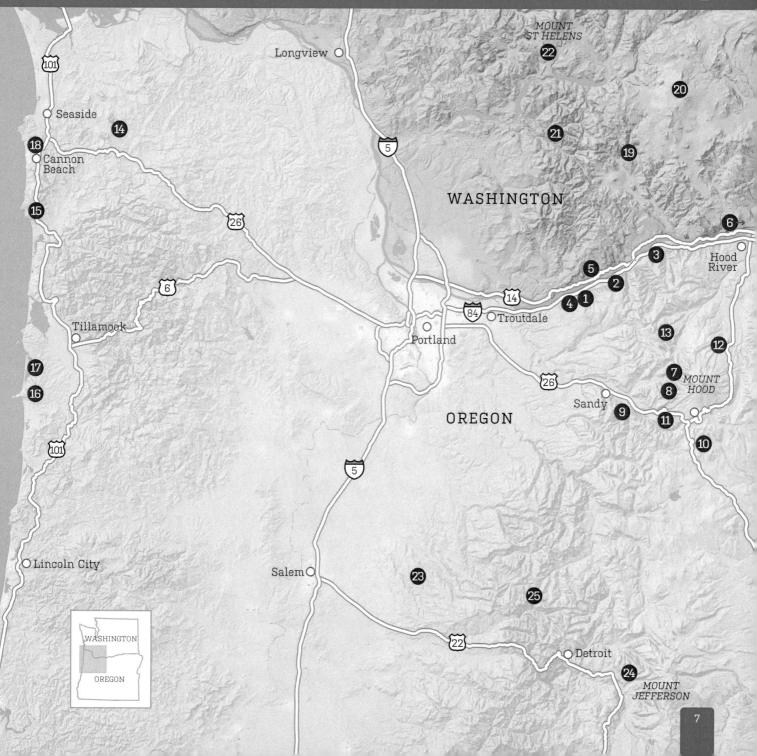

MOUNT
ST HELENS

22

20

Longview

21

101

5

19

Seaside

14

WASHINGTON

18

Cannon
Beach

6

15

3

5

Hood
River

26

2

14

4 1

84

6

Troutdale

13

Tillamook

Portland

12

17

7 MOUNT
HOOD

16

26

8

Sandy

9

101

11

OREGON

10

5

WASHINGTON

OREGON

Lincoln City

23

25

Salem

22

Detroit

24

MOUNT
JEFFERSON

Choosing a Hike

So, you want to go on a hike. How do you go about choosing where to go? This section will cover the best season for each region, including everything from a coastal hike to a secluded beach, to a high-altitude mountain alpine trek.

There are many factors to consider when choosing where to go, such as current weather conditions – including snow levels, chances of rain or snow, cloudy or sunny conditions – as well as tide times if you are heading to the coast. In addition, your current fitness level can help determine what your choices are. Are you up to a longer hike with a bit of elevation gain? Or would a shorter walk with little elevation gain be best?

COLUMBIA RIVER GORGE

While it is possible to hike in the Gorge year-round, the best time is in the spring or fall. In the spring, water levels in the creeks and waterfalls are at their highest and many varied wildflowers are in bloom alongside the trails. In autumn, the rains return to the western Gorge, and with them come more water and lush green color, as well as the fall colors of deciduous trees and understory shrubs.

Winter can be a good time to hike here, too, with far fewer crowds lending a feeling of solitude not found the rest of the year in the Gorge. The summer is a popular time for hiking anywhere, but I tend to choose to not hike in the Gorge at this time of year. All of the trails are more crowded, the landscape is drier with water levels at their lowest, and most important to me, it's prime time for hiking in the higher elevations of the mountains.

If it's a sunny spring or fall day, hikes that lead to viewpoints are a good choice. An example is **Hamilton Mountain**, with its panoramic views of the entire western Gorge. A lot of people like to head to the drier eastern part of the Gorge in the spring for early wildflowers and sunshine on hikes like the **Klickitat River Trail**. Keep an eye on weather conditions to improve your chances of basking in sunshine while everyone else is stuck in the clouds and rain.

Cloudy days are great for exploring along the creeks and waterfalls in the forests of the Gorge. Even a light rainy day can be pleasant, with impromptu waterfalls appearing on hillsides and fewer people on the trail.

Since the Columbia River Gorge spans elevations from sea level to 4,000 ft., hiking here sometimes means a lot of uphill climbing, but not always. With an elevation gain of 2,000 ft., the hike up **Hamilton Mountain** is a steep and strenuous climb. The **Wahkeena/Multnomah loop**, **Triple Falls**, and **Herman Creek Pinnacles** trails are moderately steep at times. Among the hikes in this book, the **Eagle Creek** and **Klickitat River Trail** trails offer the least amount of elevation gain.

OREGON COAST

The Oregon coast is beautiful any time of the year, so it's always a good choice on a warm, sunny day, whether it's in January or July. The key to a pleasant day at the coast is the absence of wind or rain, because days that are really windy, wet, or cloudy can feel pretty cold, regardless of the temperature.

The average annual rainfall for the Oregon coast is 75 inches, with most of the rain falling from late October to early May.

During the winter, the coast averages temperatures in the 40s - 50s. Some years, it is possible to hike at the coast in January and February in sunny 60 degree weather. Other years, it's non-stop rain, and occasionally it can even snow. Strong winter storms are common, with high winds up to 70 miles or more per hour.

In the summer, the coast is usually cooler than the rest of the state, with temperatures in the 60s and very occasionally in the 70s. It rarely gets much warmer. If there is an inland heat wave in the Willamette Valley, a condition known as advection occurs, which can bring a thick and cold fog to the coast.

Several hikes covered in this book's Oregon Coast section involve walking along beaches, including **Netarts Spit**, **Crescent Beach**, and **Indian Beach**. Know when tide times are so you don't get caught on a beach at high tide with no place to go.

Hikes on the headlands and capes of the coast offer fantastic views of the ocean while hiking through beautiful coastal rainforest. These hikes include **Cape Lookout**, **Cape Falcon**, and **Tillamook Head** at Ecola State Park.

Conditions in the Coast Range can be quite different from the coast. The **Saddle Mountain** hike is 12 miles inland from the coast, with a steep and strenuous trail to the 3,283 ft. summit. The peak commonly experiences varying weather conditions, and the trail can be icy during winter months. The best time of year in the Coast Range is typically May - June, when wildflowers are at their peak.

MOUNT HOOD, SOUTHWEST WASHINGTON AND WILLAMETTE-SANTIAM REGIONS

Hikes in mountain regions are generally only accessible from late spring to mid-autumn, with summer and early autumn being the peak season. The reason is snow. When it begins to snow and when the snow melts are the determining factors. Mosquitos also matter, because immediately after snow melt in the mountains – anywhere from late June or early July – mosquitos can be thick.

For hikes at higher elevations, August and September are premier months to hike through alpine meadows full of wildflowers, alongside alpine lakes, above tree line, and even to the base of glaciers on the mountain. This book includes higher elevation hikes to **McNeil Point**, **Jefferson Park**, and **Indian Heaven Wilderness**.

At mid-elevations in the mountains, hikes through forests full of rhododendrons, creeks and waterfalls are usually accessible by late April to early May, with flowering shrubs and wildflowers peaking through May and June. These hikes include **Ramona Falls**, **Tom Dick and Harry Mountain**, **Tamanawas Falls**, **Lost Lake Butte**, and **June Lake**.

Lower elevation hikes in these regions are snow-free earlier and include **Salmon River Canyon**, **Falls Creek Falls**, **Opal Creek**, and **Siouxon Creek**. Late April to early May is ideal with wildflowers peaking usually in early May.

Winter in the mountains is prime winter sports time, with snowshoeing a good option for hikers. The **Twins Lakes snowshoe** hike doesn't offer any views of the mountain, but it does offer more solitude than the busier sno-parks around Mount Hood.

A unique hike that is nice any time of year is Silver Falls State Park's **Trail of Ten Waterfalls**. Each season offers something different here.

WHENEVER YOU DECIDE TO GO, ENJOY TIME SPENT ON THE TRAIL!

Hiking Essentials

The level of preparation required to feel safe on a wilderness hike varies from person to person, but here are a few things all hikers should keep in mind.

THE TEN ESSENTIALS FOR HIKERS

1. Navigation: Always hike with a map indicating the trail you'll be on, preferably a topographic map that indicates changes in elevation and shows creeks and landmarks. Learn how to read the map and orient yourself. Also recommended is the use of a compass. In foggy, cloudy or snowy conditions, a compass can be the only way to navigate back to a trailhead or road for assistance. GPS units and smartphones are not substitutes for either item. Both rely on battery power and/or coverage areas in order to function.

2. Sun protection: Use sunglasses to prevent sun blindness in snow conditions and sunscreen to prevent sunburn. I like to add a hat and lip balm for sun protection.

3. Insulation: Take extra layers of clothing in case the conditions change, or in case of a need to stay overnight. Avoid cotton which when wet can remove body heat and lead to hypothermia. Wool and synthetic materials that wick moisture away from the body while retaining body heat are much better. Hiking in the Pacific Northwest means always being prepared for wet conditions, so rain gear is an essential item to take along.

4. Illumination: A headlamp or flashlight can come in handy when it takes longer than anticipated to hike out, or if needing to stay overnight.

5. First aid supplies: Take along a basic first aid kit, or assemble your own. Essential supplies include items such as bandages, tape, pain relievers, antihistamines, antibiotic ointment, and a reflective blanket. There are many good lists on the web. Google "hiking first aid kit."

6. Fire: If a need to stay overnight becomes necessary, being able to start a fire with waterproof matches is important. Lighters may not work in wet or windy conditions, or at higher elevations, so matches are a better choice. A candle can be handy for helping to get a fire going, or lighting up a small area.

7. Repair kit and tools: An all purpose Swiss Army knife or similar multi-use tool and duct tape to repair a day pack, hiking boots, etc. can be very handy.

8. Nutrition: Always take along snacks and food to cover the duration of the hike, and it's a good idea to take a bit extra in case of emergency.

9. Hydration: Take plenty of water, generally 16 ounces for a day hike, plus some type of filtration system for refilling if needed.

10. Emergency shelter: Include a reflective blanket, garbage bags, foam pads, or anything that can be used to provide protection from the elements and retain body heat.

Additional items to consider:

1. Waterproof hiking boots: These are important for stability on varied terrain, and in wet and muddy conditions.

2. Trekking poles: Used to increase stability in steep sections of trail and while crossing creeks. Many people also use trekking poles to help ease pressure on their knees.

HIKER RESPONSIBILITY CODE

Adapted from the HikeSafe.com website, this set of principles was created to help hikers become more self aware about their responsibility for their own safety every time they are on a hike.

Be responsible and be prepared:

1. With knowledge and gear. Become self reliant by learning about the terrain, conditions, local weather, and your equipment before you start.

2. To leave your plans. Tell someone where you are going, the trails you are hiking, when you will return, and your emergency plans.

3. To stay together. When you start as a group, hike as a group, end as a group. Pace your hike to the slowest person.

4. To turn back. Weather changes quickly. Fatigue and unexpected conditions can also affect your hike. Know your limitations and when to postpone your hike. The trail will be there another day.

5. For emergencies. Even if you are headed out for just an hour, an injury, severe weather or a wrong turn could become life threatening. Don't assume you will be rescued; know how to rescue yourself.

6. To share the hiker code with others.

To learn more, visit **hikesafe.com**.

LEAVE NO TRACE

The basis for the Leave No Trace principle is to leave nature in the same or better condition than you found it.

1. Use established trails: Don't create new paths or cut-throughs which add to the amount of trail maintenance done by not only our national and state parks crews, but also by many volunteers.

2. Leave it: Leave what you find in place, including wildflowers and vegetation. Some wildflowers depend on the current plants to regenerate and picking them can cause them to die out.

3. Pack it out. If you brought it in, be sure to pack it out. Don't leave anything behind, including tissues, food, plastic, etc. Even if labeled biodegradable, it can take years for things to decompose.

4. Wildlife: Don't feed wildlife, which creates dependency and unhealthy habits, as well as a nuisance. Bears, chipmunks, and other animals aren't as cute when they rummage through your pack or campsite for food and won't leave you alone. Teach your children to respect nature by not interfering with it.

To learn more, visit **www.lnt.org**.

Geological History of the Area

One of the many reasons to love the Pacific Northwest is its diverse physical beauty. And much of that beauty is due to the region's geological history.

By Kaitlyn Allegretti

Geology provides much of the visual appeal of hiking, with its variations in rock formations, elegant waterfalls, and fertile soils that provide an ideal environment for various flora and fauna.

But where do these geologic variations come from? Why does the Indian Heaven Wilderness look so vastly different from Hamilton Mountain? Or why can hikers pass through an amphitheater of eroded soft sediment behind Silver Falls, while viewing Ramona Falls means standing at the base of a cascading staircase of fractured columnar basalt?

This section of the book aims to present a brief history of the region, and provide a basic understanding of the geologic splendor that is the Pacific Northwest.

Covered by basalt lava flows and carved by the Missoula Floods at the end of the last ice age, the Columbia River Gorge cuts through the Cascade mountains between the states of Oregon and Washington.

To understand the geologic history of an area, it is important to consider the many processes that have occurred throughout time, which have created the features that we see today.

PLATE TECTONICS

Looking back to a time more than 4.5 billion years ago, this process began with the formation of the earth. When it was first formed, the earth's crust cooled slowly, which created a patchwork of landforms that looked and worked like puzzle pieces. These puzzle pieces are called tectonic plates. Over millions of years, these plates have moved slowly across the earth's surface, and continue to do so today.

There are two major types of tectonic plates – continental and oceanic. Where two plates meet is referred to as a plate boundary.

The Pacific Northwest lies adjacent to a convergent plate boundary, which is a boundary where two plates approach each other and collide. The less dense oceanic plate (Juan de Fuca) sinks below the more dense continental plate (North American). This action creates an area referred to as a subduction zone.

In the context of the geologic history of the earth, Oregon and Washington are rather young. They are "add-ons" to the original coastal edge of the North American plate, which formerly ended near the Idaho border.

The bedrock of the Pacific Northwest was formed by a combination of the North American plate moving westward, the subduction of oceanic plates moving eastward, and the cementing together of exotic terranes onto the edge of the continent through a

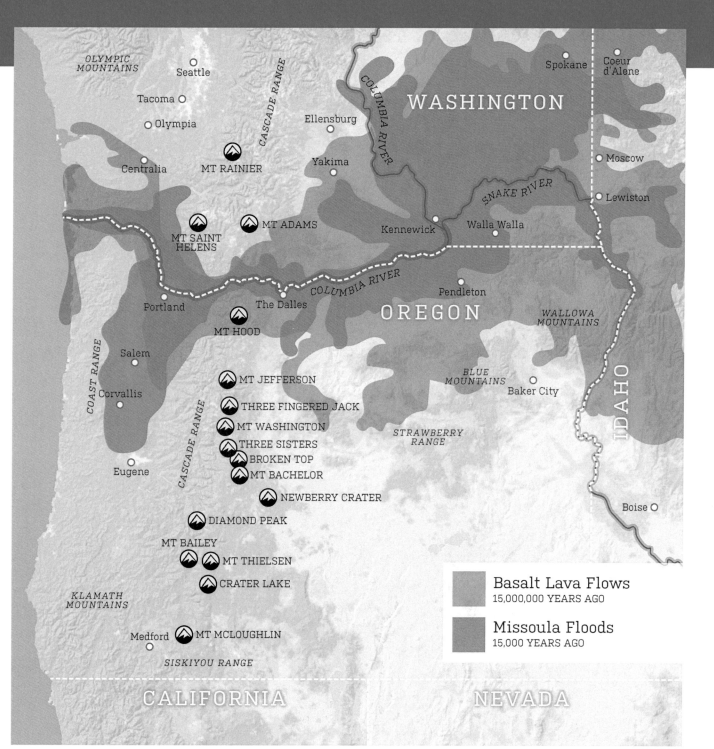

Basalt Lava Flows
15,000,000 YEARS AGO

Missoula Floods
15,000 YEARS AGO

process called accretion. The exotic terranes are blocks of the earth's crust that formed in a different place and time, then drifted across the Pacific basin and collided with the North American Plate during the subduction of the oceanic plate.

As the Juan de Fuca plate goes through the subduction process, it does not simply disappear. Instead, it partially melts, forming molten magma, generating steam and gas, and creating the volcanic archipelago of the Cascade Mountains. And this process is still happening today, which continues to feed the area's active volcanic arc.

Year after year, the topography of the Pacific Northwest is changing, continuing the processes that began millions of years ago. Over time, these changes have resulted in periods of crustal creation and uplift, volcanism and earthquakes, varying climates, the rise and fall of sea level, phases of glaciation, and cataclysmic floods causing large amounts of erosion and deposition.

That's a long list of amazing developments, but what does that mean in practical terms? What exactly can be seen when hiking in this area?

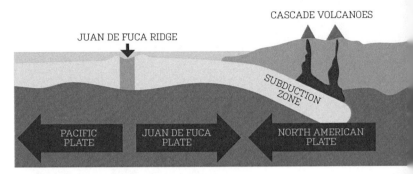

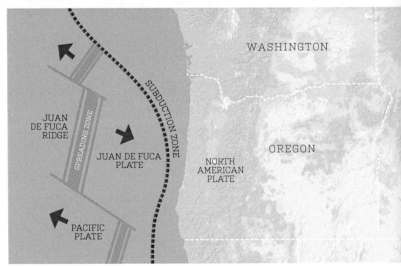

VOLCANOES

Something all hikers notice are the snow-capped peaks of the Cascades. The volcanic Cascade Mountain range spans from southern British Columbia to northern California. As the dominate visual features of the region, Mount Rainier, Mount St. Helens, Mount Adams, Mount Hood and Mount Jefferson, all of which are stratovolcanoes, tower over the surrounding peaks of the range.

Stratovolcanoes, also referred to as composite volcanoes, are formed from numerous eruption periods. As these eruptions occur, layers of basalt, andesite, and dacite lavas and ash are created, which then harden into steep slopes.

These volcanoes all contain rocks that formed within the last 40,000 to 500,000 years, and it's easy to believe that they're still active. Mount St. Helens experienced an explosive eruption as recently as 1980, and has continued to display some volcanic activity within the past decade.

ICE

In addition to volcanoes, ice played a significant role in shaping the Cascades. Less than 100,000 years ago, ice sheets modified the surface of the Cascades while lavas continued to erupt both above and below the ice, creating a landscape of fire and ice. Numerous alpine glaciers remain from the last major glacial event, continuing to erode the surface of these volcanoes today and supply the rivers with their melt water.

And finally, add floods to the list of geologic influencers. Two major flood events are associated with the Columbia River.

FLOODS

Roughly 15 million years ago, fissures (large cracks) opened in western Idaho, eastern Oregon, and eastern Washington, erupting with fast moving lavas that are referred to as the Columbia River Basalts. In geology, these lava floods are known as basalt flows.

Then approximately 15 thousand years ago, a lake called Glacial Lake Missoula broke through an ice dam, releasing over 500 cubic miles of water. These water floods are known as the Missoula Floods.

Over 300 basalt flows and up to 100 glacial floods left behind deposits at various termination points, with some flows reaching the Pacific Ocean. Envision standing on the summit of Saddle Mountain in the Coast Range and looking east, knowing that the upper unit of that mountain originated more than 300 miles away in eastern Washington.

The erosional forces from the glacial floods were immense. They transformed the V-shaped valley of the Columbia River into its present day U-shaped valley, leaving behind an abundance of waterfalls.

Geology is always telling a story and providing a lens to the history of the world, both in the context of months or a over a timeline of millions of years. And the landscape of the Pacific Northwest provides ample opportunities to view an assortment of geologic features and processes.

Multiple layers of basalt flows are visible in the vertical cliffs at Multnomah Falls.

ABOUT THE GEOLOGY CONTRIBUTOR

Kaitlyn grew up in Pennsylvania, where she spent her days playing outside and picking up rocks. This love for the natural world led Kaitlyn to study geology at the University of Dayton. Following college, she moved to the Pacific Northwest and has resided in the Portland area since 2009. Kaitlyn has over five years of experience as an environmental scientist, and enjoys the ongoing education and field time required for her job.

Outside of work, Kaitlyn continues to enjoy spending time at the coast and on the mountains, among the trees, rocks and waters of the area. Aside from geology driven adventures, she enjoys cooking, traveling and the perks of Portland.

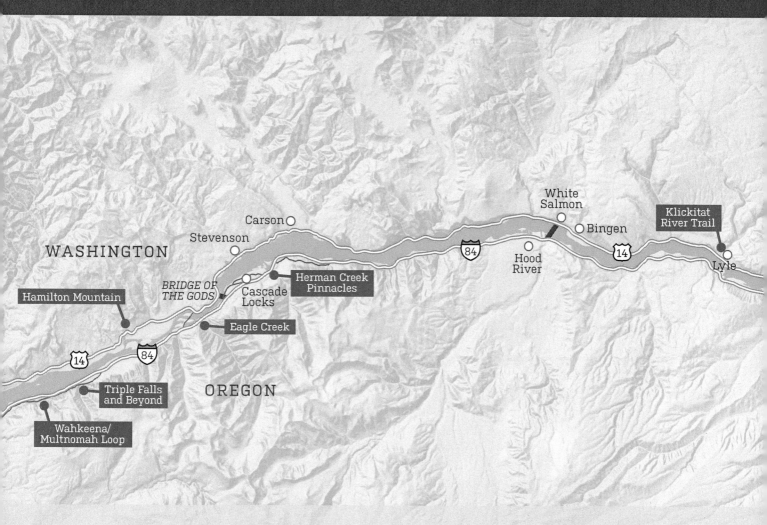

The only sea-level route through the Cascade Mountains, the Columbia River Gorge is a source of outstanding natural beauty that was designated as a National Scenic Area in 1986. The Gorge features scenery ranging from the western portion's misty mountains, lush forests and more waterfalls than any single place in the U.S., to the eastern section's drier environment with rolling hills and rim-rock bluffs. This environmental diversity is due to the extreme variability of elevation and precipitation. The Gorge is 85 miles wide, with elevations rising from sea level to as high as 4,000 ft. And the amount of rainfall varies from an average of less than 15 inches annually in the eastern Gorge, to an average of 75 inches annually in the western Gorge.

Triple Falls and Beyond

Four waterfalls, a narrow slot canyon, viewpoints overlooking the Columbia River, two cascading creeks, plus moss and ferns covering everything in sight make this hike one of the best in the Columbia River Gorge.

DIRECTIONS

From Portland, take I-84 East for 25 miles to the Bridal Veil Exit 28.

Follow the off ramp to the intersection with the Historic Highway and turn left (east).

Drive 5.6 miles. (2.5 miles past Multnomah Falls Lodge) to a small parking lot on the left, directly across from Horsetail Falls.

For an alternate route that bypasses the Multnomah Falls crowds, drive an additional 7 miles on I-84 and take the next exit, Ainsworth Exit 35. At the stop sign turn left (west) towards Multnomah Falls on the Historic Hwy for 1.6 miles to the trailhead.

Drive time from Portland: 40 minutes

THE HIKE

Begin at the Horsetail trailhead, located directly next to Horsetail Falls (176 ft.). The first portion of the hike switchbacks up from the highway, gaining about 400 feet in 0.3 miles. After a section of mossy rock and views of the Columbia River, the trail heads inward to go behind Ponytail Falls (80 ft.), also known as Upper Horsetail Falls. The lava flow that created the falls covered soft soil, which over time has been washed away, creating the cavern behind the falls. From Ponytail Falls, continue another .25 miles to side trails that lead to great cliff-edge views of the Columbia River.

As the main trail begins a downward section of switchbacks, stop at a viewpoint looking down into the narrow 20 ft. wide slot canyon of Oneonta Gorge. Upon reaching the metal bridge over Oneonta Creek, Middle Oneonta Falls (24 ft.) is to the left. To the right, the creek drops off a ledge to unseen Lower Oneonta Falls (120 ft.). In late summer when water levels are at their lowest, it is possible to wade up the creek from the Oneonta trailhead to the base of this waterfall.

At the trail junction with Oneonta Trail 424, turn left to head to Triple Falls. (Shorter loop option: turn right to go back to the highway. This option results in a .25 mile walk along the road to return to the parking lot.) The trail to Triple Falls continues to gain elevation and is rocky and steep in a few spots. At Triple Falls (64 ft.), a side trail on the left leads to a closer view from a rocky slope directly across from the three-channel waterfall. The main trail continues on the right to a large wooden bridge that crosses the creek and enters a scenic area heavily covered with ferns, moss and lichens, making it look much like a fairyland. The trail is creekside for the next mile, with plenty of spots for observing or exploring alongside the creek.

After another mile, a small log bridge crosses the creek and everything becomes even more green than before. Continue to a trail junction and a clearing next to the creek for the final destination. Return the same way.

Distance: 6.4 miles (roundtrip)

Elevation Gain: 1,200 ft.

Difficulty: Moderate

Hike type: out and back

Trail: packed dirt and rock

Typical open: all year, but may be icy during the winter

Best time of year: April - June and Oct. - Nov.

Features: waterfalls, creeks, forest

Fees/permits: none required

Agency: Columbia River Gorge National Scenic Area (see pg. 126)

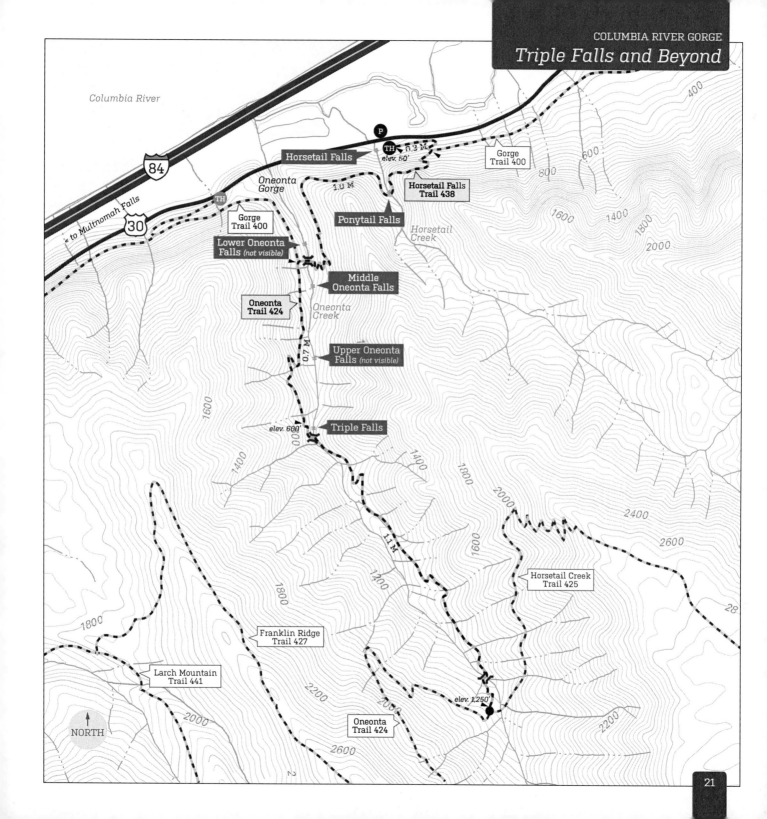

Columbia River

84

Oneonta Gorge

30

← to Multnomah Falls

P

TH

Horsetail Falls

0.2 M

elev. 50'

Gorge Trail 400

1.0 M

Horsetail Falls Trail 438

Ponytail Falls

Horsetail Creek

TH

Gorge Trail 400

Lower Oneonta Falls *(not visible)*

Middle Oneonta Falls

Oneonta Trail 424

Oneonta Creek

Upper Oneonta Falls *(not visible)*

0.7 M

elev. 600'

Triple Falls

1.1 M

Horsetail Creek Trail 425

Franklin Ridge Trail 427

elev. 1,250'

Larch Mountain Trail 441

Oneonta Trail 424

NORTH

Eagle Creek to High Bridge ②

Along this three mile stretch of the extremely popular Eagle Creek trail with its steep cliff walls are three spectacular waterfalls, cascading side creeks and a narrow slot canyon.

DIRECTIONS

Take I-84 east for 38 miles to the Eagle Creek Recreation Area Exit 41.

Turn right and drive 0.5 miles to the trailhead.

Drive time from Portland: 45 minutes

THE HIKE

Built in 1915, the same year the historic Columbia Highway opened, the Eagle Creek trail is an engineering marvel. It was built using pick-axes and shovels, with sections of the trail blasted out of the vertical rock. The first several miles of trail have an easy grade with little elevation gain and plenty of spectacular scenery along the way. The hike begins at the base of the Eagle Creek canyon with towering basalt walls. The first section gently climbs through a forest of oak, big-leaf maple, cedar and Douglas fir before approaching the first of several sections of trail with steep drop-offs to the side and hand rails along the ledge. There is plenty of room on the trail, but it's easy for those afraid of heights to get a bit nervous, especially if you look down at the creek several hundred feet below.

At about one mile in, there's a short side trail to a viewpoint of Metlako Falls (82 ft.), which is named after the Native American goddess of salmon. After crossing a bridge with views of a scenic and mossy rock-lined side creek, a marked side trail for Punch Bowl Falls descends to an open rocky area along the creek beside Lower Punch Bowl Falls (12 ft.). Just around the bend is the base of the famous Punch Bowl Falls (36 ft.) waterfall, plunging into its rocky circular bowl. Back on the main trail, just beyond the Punch Bowl side trail, is a view of this waterfall from high above, which makes for a good resting point. The next mile of trail crosses another small bridge over a lovely cascading side creek and passes through a large rockslide.

As the trail nears High Bridge, wispy two-tiered Loowit Falls (93 ft.) can be seen across a steep, narrow gorge. The first tier cascades about 90 feet into a small pool, with the second tier falling several more feet into the creek. Just ahead is High Bridge, a wide metal bridge spanning 120 feet above a slot canyon. There are plenty of areas to sit and enjoy the scenery before heading back. Return the same way.

Distance: 6.6 miles (roundtrip)

Elevation Gain: 600 feet

Difficulty: easy to moderate

Hike type: out and back

Trail: packed dirt and rock

Typical open: all year, but may be icy during the winter

Best time of year: April - June and Oct. - Nov.

Features: waterfalls, forest, creek

Fees/permits: none

Agency: Columbia River Gorge National Scenic Area (see pg. 126)

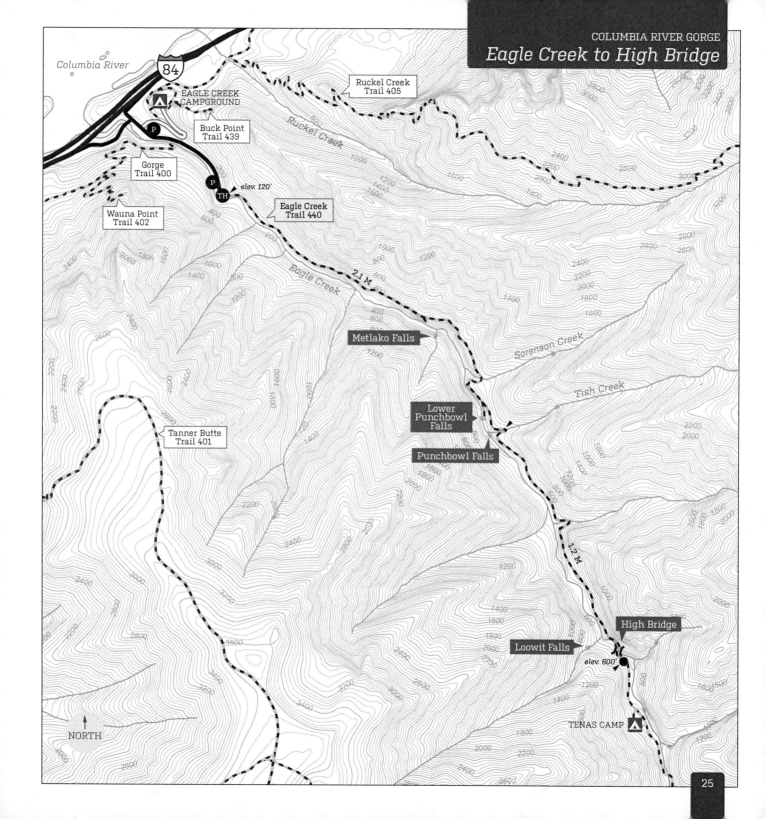

Columbia River

84

EAGLE CREEK CAMPGROUND

Buck Point Trail 439

Gorge Trail 400

P

TH *elev. 120'*

Wauna Point Trail 402

Eagle Creek Trail 440

Eagle Creek

Ruckel Creek Trail 405

Ruckel Creek

2.1 M

Metlako Falls

Sorenson Creek

Tish Creek

Lower Punchbowl Falls

Tanner Butte Trail 401

Punchbowl Falls

1.2 M

High Bridge

Loowit Falls

elev. 600'

TENAS CAMP

NORTH

Herman Creek Pinnacles

3

The basalt monoliths on this hike aren't the only interesting feature: a metal footbridge over lovely Herman Creek, wispy Pacific Crest Falls, and a mossy section of lava boulders add to the appeal.

DIRECTIONS

From Portland, drive east on I-84 for 40 miles to Cascade Locks exit 44.

Continue through the town of Cascade Locks.

Under the freeway, continue east on the Frontage Road on the south side of the highway for about 2 more miles to Herman Creek Campground.

Turn right, going uphill into the campground, and stay to the right to the day use area parking lot.

If the road to the campground is gated, park next to the frontage road and walk up the campground road.

Drive time from Portland: 1 hour

THE HIKE

This hike begins in a mixed forest of Douglas fir and bigleaf maple trees covered heavily with lichens and moss. After crossing uphill to an open power line section, stay to the right on the path and continue on the trail through a bit more forest before encountering a stretch of moss covered boulders, some with cave-like openings at their base which look like they could be home to elves, trolls or other forest folk.

At a signed trail junction, fork to the right on the Herman Creek Bridge Trail. Heading downhill towards Herman Creek, which you can hear below you for quite a distance, the trail crosses a long metal footbridge, which offers great views of Herman Creek in both directions. This is the only time you'll be near the creek, so it's worth spending a few minutes taking in the views from the bridge or exploring the banks of the creek below.

About one mile from the creek, turn right on the Pacific Crest Trail (PCT), a 2,650 mile trail that runs from Mexico to Canada through California, Oregon, and Washington. Continue through alternating forested and rocky talus slopes, with occasional openings to views of the Columbia River and the Washington side of the Gorge, to Pacific Crest Falls, a wispy waterfall that cascades down the hillside above and below the trail.

In early spring, the water flow is at its peak, making the waterfall a nice feature of this hike. Continue on the trail for about 250 yards to the pinnacles. A small rocky path leads to a nice open area at the base of the spires. Spend a bit of time exploring around the spires – there are several small paths leading up and around the bases of these fascinating structures.

Optional longer hike: in another 1.3 miles is Dry Creek Falls, a relatively unknown waterfall that is anything but dry. Return the same way.

Distance: 4.8 miles (roundtrip)

Elevation Gain: 1,020 feet

Difficulty: moderate

Hike type: out and back

Trail: packed dirt

Typical open: all year, but may be icy during the winter

Best time of year: April - June and Oct. - Nov.

Features: forest, creek, waterfall, geologic features

Fees/permits: Northwest Forest Pass required

Agency: Columbia River Gorge National Scenic Area (see pg. 126)

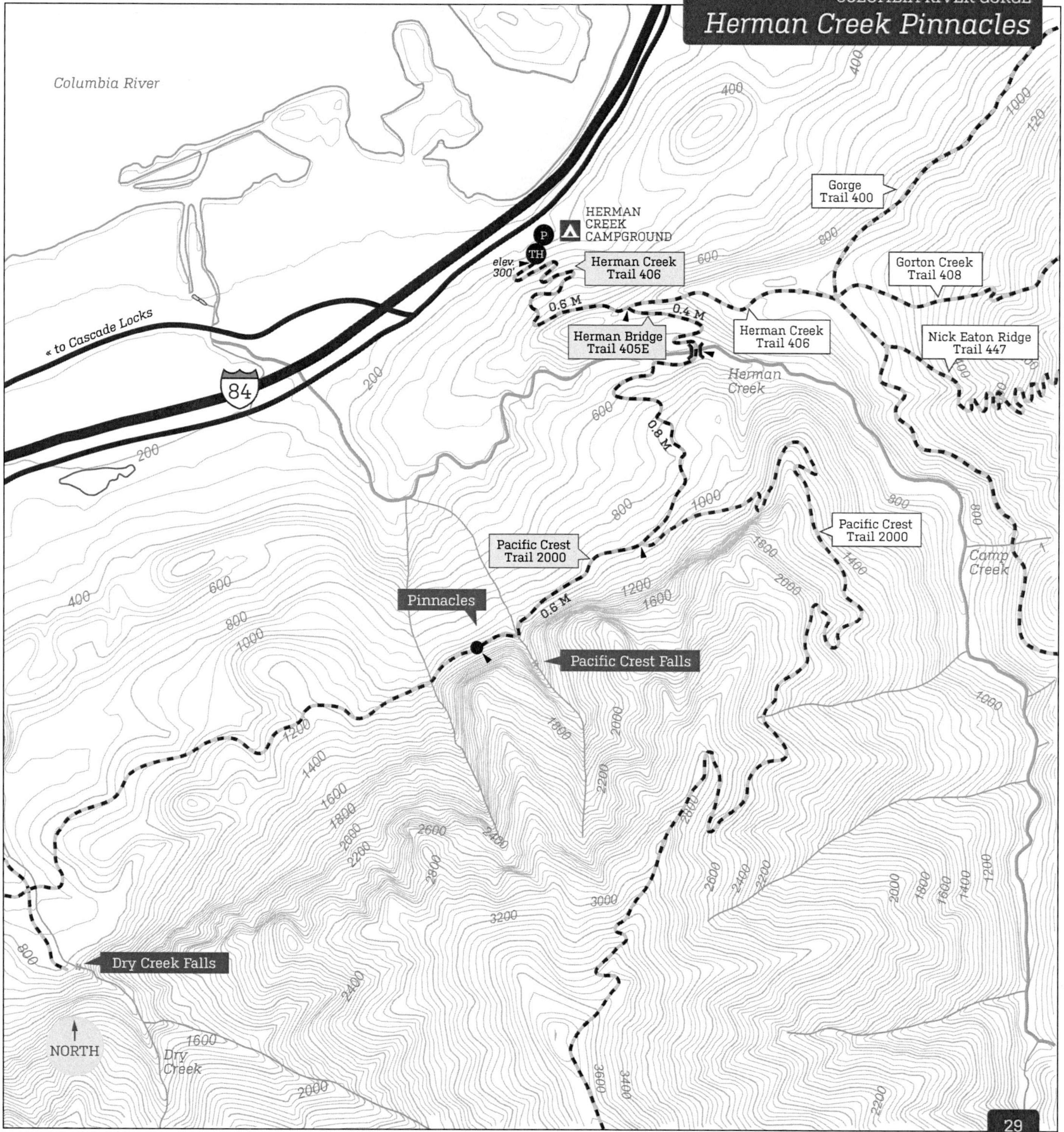

Columbia River

HERMAN
CREEK
CAMPGROUND

P

TH

elev.
300'

Herman Creek
Trail 406

0.6 M

0.4 M

Herman Bridge
Trail 405E

Herman Creek
Trail 406

Herman
Creek

Gorge
Trail 400

Gorton Creek
Trail 408

Nick Eaton Ridge
Trail 447

« to Cascade Locks

84

0.8 M

Pacific Crest
Trail 2000

Pacific Crest
Trail 2000

Camp
Creek

Pinnacles

0.6 M

Pacific Crest Falls

Dry Creek Falls

NORTH

Dry
Creek

29

Wahkeena/Multnomah Falls Loop

4

Despite the crowds, six waterfalls, including Oregon's highest, two picturesque cascading spring-fed creeks meandering through lush greenery, and old-growth Douglas fir make this a spectacular loop hike.

DIRECTIONS

From Portland, take I-84 East for 25 miles to the Bridal Veil Exit 28.

Follow the off ramp to the intersection with the Historic Highway and turn left.

Drive 2.5 miles to the parking lot for the Wahkeena Falls trailhead.

Drive time from Portland: 35 minutes

THE HIKE

Wahkeena is a Yakima Native American word meaning "most beautiful," which is quite appropriate for this creek and waterfall. Beginning at the Wahkeena Falls trailhead, cross the small stone bridge over the creek and begin a series of switchbacks on paved trail to a footbridge at the base of Wahkeena Falls (242 ft.). The height of the falls can seem deceptive because instead of falling in one plunge, it falls in a series of tiers, some of which are difficult to see from the trail. After several more switchbacks, you'll reach Lemmon's Viewpoint, with views of the Columbia River and across to Washington.

All along the uphill sections of trail, Wahkeena Creek rushes downhill, cascading through mossy rock next to ferns, berries and many wildflowers in the spring. One of the loveliest of waterfalls along the hike, delicate Fairy Falls (20 ft.) cascades over a blocky basalt rock wall. To see the springs that appear from underground and are the source of Wahkeena Creek, turn right at the Angels Rest trail junction for about 100 yards. This is a scenic area, with the springs bubbling up from below ground, then pooling and meandering beneath large trees before heading downhill.

Return to the Wahkeena trail and head uphill, crossing a heavily wooded slope for about 1.5 miles before reaching the canyon of Multnomah Creek. The first waterfall along this section is Ecola Falls (55 ft.). Wiesendanger Falls (50 ft.) drops over a flat ledge of the creek into a rocky bowl. Just ahead on the trail is Dutchman's Tunnel, an overhang of basalt that creates a cave-like structure with tiny plants hanging down from the rock crevices. Dutchman Falls is a succession of three short falls along the creek just before a side trail to the overlook for Multnomah Falls. A two-tiered waterfall, Multnomah Falls (620 ft.) is the highest waterfall in Oregon. With five different flows of lava visible in the rock face of Multnomah Falls, this is a good place to see evidence of the Gorge's geological history. At the base of the falls is the historic Multnomah Lodge, built in 1915 around the same time as the historic Columbia highway. Next to the lodge, take the roadside trail back to the Wahkeena Falls parking area.

Distance: 5.4 miles (roundtrip)

Elevation Gain: 1,600 ft.

Difficulty: moderate

Hike type: loop

Trail: asphalt and packed dirt

Typical open: all year, but may be icy during the winter

Best time of year: April - June and Oct. - Nov.

Features: waterfalls, creeks, forest

Fees/permits: none

Agency: Columbia River Gorge National Scenic Area (see pg. 126)

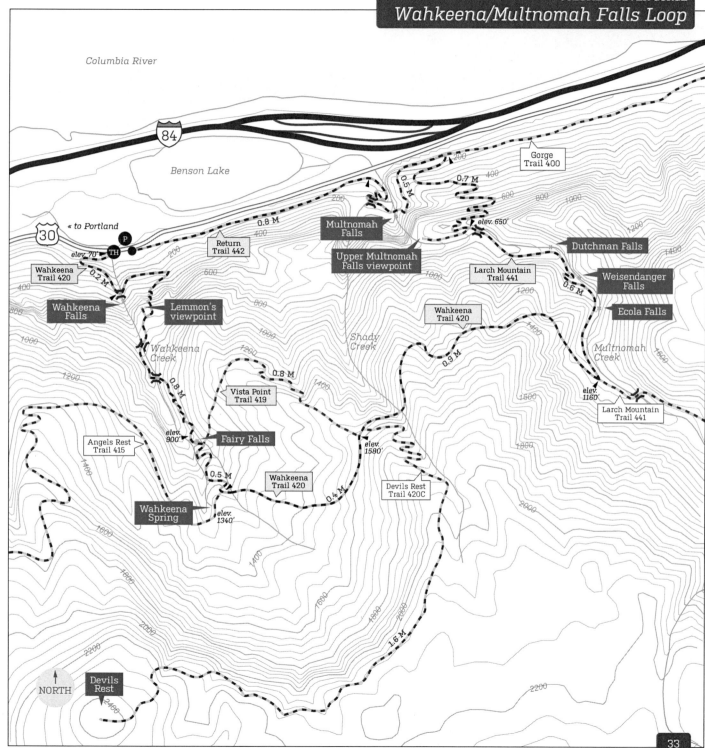

Columbia River

84

Benson Lake

Gorge
Trail 400

0.5 M

0.7 M

elev. 650'

30 « to Portland

0.8 M

Multnomah
Falls

Dutchman Falls

Return
Trail 442

Upper Multnomah
Falls viewpoint

Larch Mountain
Trail 441

Weisendanger
Falls

elev. 70'
TH
P

Wahkeena
Trail 420

0.2 M

Ecola Falls

Wahkeena
Falls

Lemmon's
viewpoint

Wahkeena
Trail 420

0.9 M

Multnomah
Creek

Wahkeena
Creek

Shady
Creek

0.8 M

Vista Point
Trail 419

elev.
1160'

Larch Mountain
Trail 441

0.8 M

elev.
900'

Angels Rest
Trail 415

Fairy Falls

elev.
1580'

0.5 M

Wahkeena
Trail 420

0.4 M

Devils Rest
Trail 420C

Wahkeena
Spring

elev.
1340'

1.6 M

NORTH

Devils
Rest

Climb a steep rocky trail past two waterfalls, leading up to a high peak on the Columbia River Gorge with astonishing panoramic views of the Columbia River and the Oregon side of the Gorge.

DIRECTIONS

From Portland, drive east on I-84 to exit 44 for Cascade Locks.

Turn right at the sign for Bridge of the Gods.

Go across the bridge, paying $1 toll, and turn left onto Highway 14.

Drive west for 6.6 miles to Beacon Rock State Park, and make a sharp right turn into the day use parking lot.

Drive time from Portland: 1 hour

THE HIKE

Beginning at a picnic area with a pavilion built in the 1930s by the Civilian Conservation Corps, the trail begins in the forest before briefly passing through an open area with power lines. There's a good view here of Hamilton Mountain and the ridge below it.

At a sign for Hardy Falls, take the side trail all the way down several sections of steps to the end of a platform that overlooks Hardy Creek as it cascades down the hillside. Back on the main trail, a short distance ahead, the second major waterfall in this area is Rodney Falls. A short side trail goes up to the Pool of Winds, where Hardy Creek plunges into a rocky cave-like structure. Constant strong winds and sprays of water from the rush of the creek give this falls its name. Cross over a long boardwalk bridge, with the water of the creek splashing beneath the bridge.

Several switchbacks of stairs climb up the hillside, and from here on, the trail gets much steeper. A trail junction connects the Hardy Ridge loop to Hamilton Mountain, but most people continue straight either for the cliff ridge section, or to the summit of Hamilton, using the optional route on the way back. The cliff ridge area is about .25 miles from the junction. To get up to the ridge, climb a very steep path in about the middle of the ridge. At the top, take in at the amazing panoramic views, being careful of the sheer drop-offs.

To get to the summit of Hamilton, continue straight on the trail for another 1.5 miles through a series of switchbacks. The view from the top is only open to the east, looking towards Table Mountain and Mount Adams.

For a longer 9 mile loop on a much less steep route, when leaving the summit, go along a saddle behind Hamilton and down to an old jeep road until arriving at a sign that leads back to the main trail. Back at the junction to Hamilton Mountain, turn right and go back the way you came, passing the waterfalls again.

Distance: 7.6 miles (roundtrip)

Elevation Gain: 2,000 feet

Difficulty: difficult

Hike type: out and back, with loop options

Trail: packed dirt and rock

Features: waterfalls, creeks, forest, views

Typical open: March - Nov.

Best time of year: April -June

Fees: Washington Discover Pass

Agency: Washington State Parks: Beacon Rock State Park (see pg. 126)

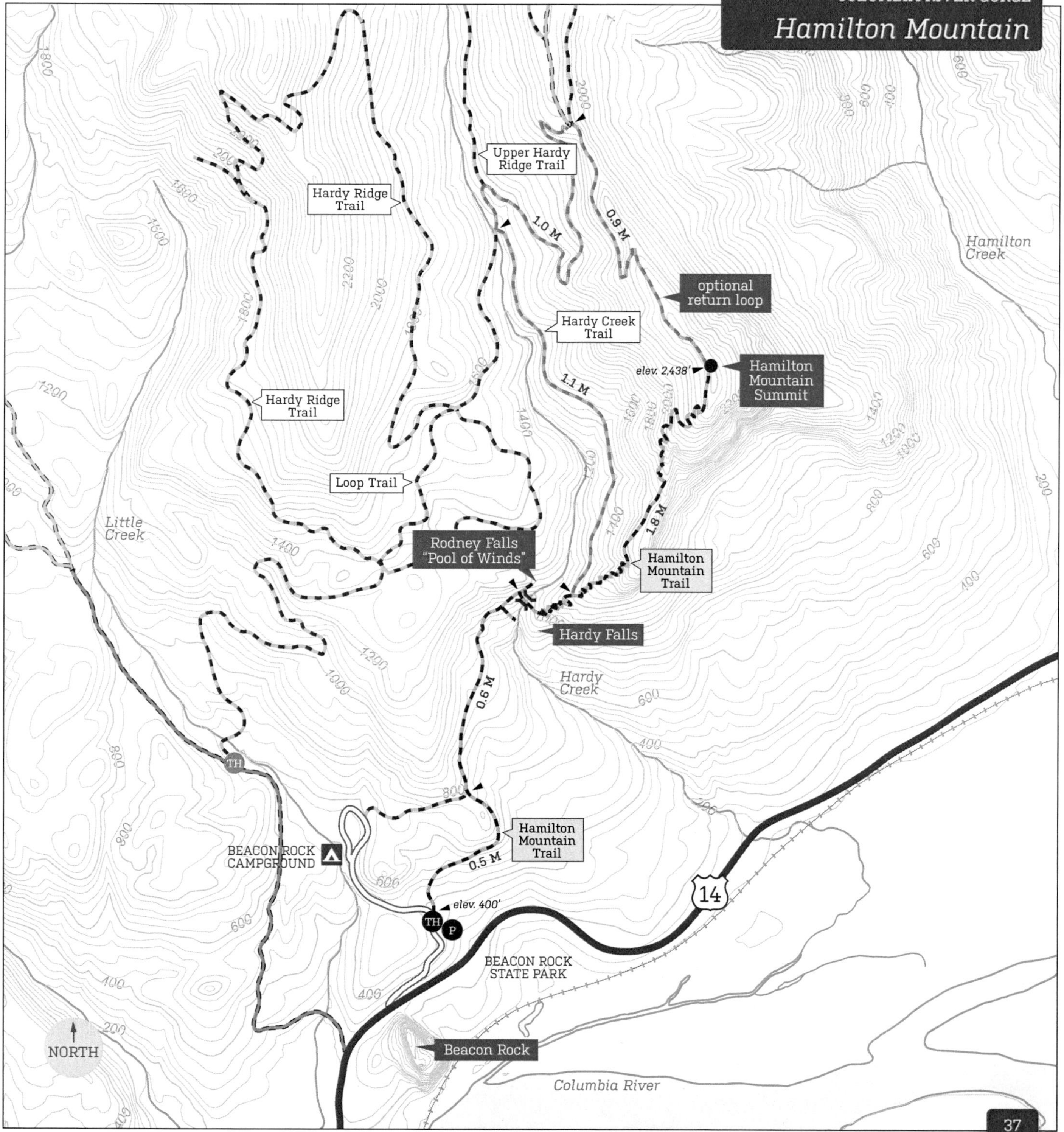

Upper Hardy
Ridge Trail

Hardy Ridge
Trail

1.0 M

0.9 M

optional
return loop

Hardy Creek
Trail

Hardy Ridge
Trail

1.1 M

elev. 2,438'

Hamilton
Mountain
Summit

Loop Trail

1.8 M

Rodney Falls
"Pool of Winds"

Little
Creek

Hamilton
Mountain
Trail

Hardy Falls

Hardy
Creek

0.6 M

TH

BEACON ROCK
CAMPGROUND

Hamilton
Mountain
Trail

0.5 M

14

elev. 400'

TH P

BEACON ROCK
STATE PARK

NORTH

Beacon Rock

Columbia River

In the spring when it's still cloudy and rainy in Portland, head east to the sunny and drier environment of the Eastern Columbia River Gorge, an area that looks much like the wild west of old movies.

DIRECTIONS

From Portland, drive east on I-84 to exit 44 for Cascade Locks.

Turn right at the sign for Bridge of the Gods.

Go across the bridge, paying $1 toll, and turn right onto Highway 14.

Continue on Hwy 14 for about 35 miles to WA-142.

Turn left and park at the Lyle Trailhead parking area for the Klickitat Trail.

Drive time from Portland: 1 hour 30 minutes

THE HIKE

The Klickitat River Trail is a 31-mile former rail corridor that runs along the Wild and Scenic Klickitat River where it meets the Columbia River in Lyle, Washington and then heads up the isolated Swale Canyon before ending near Warwick, Washington. This section of the hike is known as the Lower Klickitat River Trail and is open to hikers and bikers. Due to excessive heat in the summer, the trail is only open from October - June. Bald eagles congregate here in January and February to take advantage of winter salmon runs.

In early spring, the normally brown hills all around are greener, and colors from abundant Deer brush (a shrub with many sprays of light blue to purplish flowers), Columbia desert parsley, and yellow Northwestern balsomroot lend beauty to this "wild west" feeling canyon filled with stands of ponderosa pine, oak trees, and rocky rims. Keep an eye out for poison oak and rattlesnakes, and be prepared for ticks. Along the trail, mile markers help keep track of each mile of trail with metal signposts.

The first 1.5 miles of the trail is an old gravel road bed, which runs very close to Highway 142. Fishermen's access trails lead down to the river with great views of the canyon, but they don't connect back to the hiking trail. Native Americans still use traditional dip net fishing methods here during salmon season, fishing from platforms perched along the rocky sides of the river.

Crossing the river, the Fisher Hill pedestrian bridge spans the Klickitat as it churns through a narrow rocky gorge. From here on, the trail is on the opposite side of the river from the highway and is much more secluded and scenic. Pass the Lyle Falls facility where salmon put on a show attempting to jump the 8-foot waterfall in September. Continue on the trail, passing a water flow measurement raft moored on the opposite bank of the river. The canyon narrows, with basalt cliffs rising on the side of the trail, and the river widens creating rapids in the fast moving water. Cross a boardwalk through a tunnel of white alders and continue to the 4 mile marker before returning the same way.

Distance: 8 miles (roundtrip)

Elevation Gain: 125 ft.

Difficulty: easy

Hike type: out and back

Trail: old road bed and packed dirt

Features: river, Native American fishing platforms, sunny skies

Typical open: Oct. - June

Best time of year: April - May

Fees: none

Agency: Washington State Parks (see pg. 126)

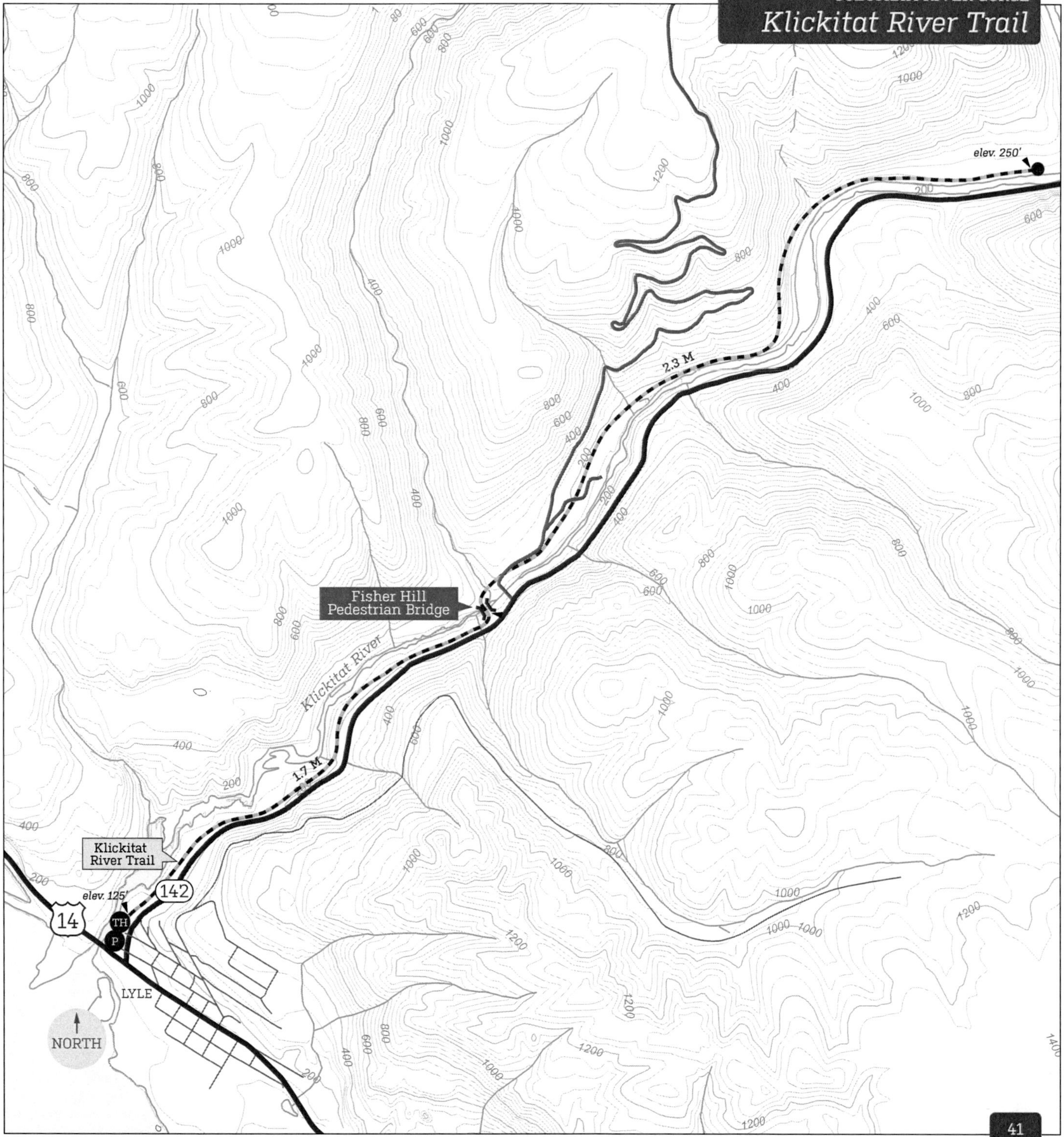

elev. 250'

2.3 M

Fisher Hill
Pedestrian Bridge

Klickitat River

1.7 M

Klickitat
River Trail

elev. 125'

142

14

TH
P

LYLE

NORTH

41

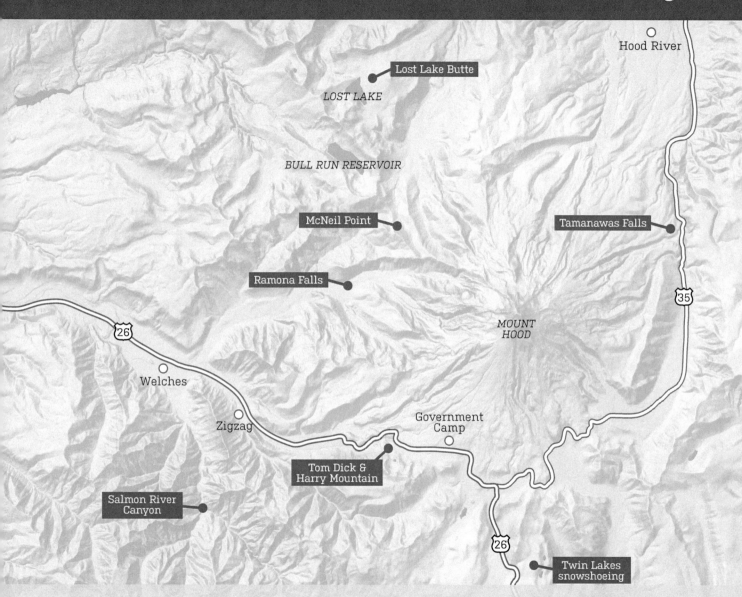

Hood River

Lost Lake Butte

LOST LAKE

BULL RUN RESERVOIR

McNeil Point

Tamanawas Falls

Ramona Falls

35

MOUNT HOOD

26

Welches

Zigzag

Government Camp

Tom Dick & Harry Mountain

Salmon River Canyon

26

Twin Lakes snowshoeing

At 11,249 ft., Mount Hood is Oregon's highest mountain and the fourth highest in the Cascade range. A dormant volcano, Mount Hood's last major eruption was around 300 years ago. It is considered a likely candidate to become active again. With nearly 1,000 miles of trails in the region, hikes range from lower elevation rambles in mossy forest with waterfalls and creeks to high mountain alpine trails that reach above timberline on the mountain.

Hike along the Bald Mountain ridge on Mount Hood's northwest side, passing through wildflower-filled alpine meadows to the McNeil Point stone shelter.

DIRECTIONS

From Portland: drive 42 miles east on U.S. 26 to Zigzag.

Across from the Zigzag Ranger District, turn left onto East Lolo Pass Road.

Travel for 4.2 miles, then fork right on paved road 1825.

After 0.7 miles, just before a bridge over the Sandy River, go straight on Road 1828 (paved single lane road with turnouts).

Continue 5.6 miles and fork to the right on gravel Road 118, for 1.5 miles to the Top Spur Trailhead.

Drive time from Portland: 1 hour 40 minutes

THE HIKE

Starting at the Top Spur trailhead, the first several miles are in a Douglas fir and mountain hemlock cathedral forest, with an understory of huckleberries that ripen in August. Less than a quarter-mile from the trailhead, turn right at the junction with the Pacific Crest Trail, and at a three-trail junction a short distance later, bear left (somewhat uphill) on the Timberline Trail. An optional (center) trail loops around Bald Mountain, providing big views of Mount Hood and adding just under a half-mile to the hike. A short distance ahead, fill out a wilderness permit at the self-registration station.

Continue on the Timberline Trail to the wildflower-filled slopes of Bald Mountain Ridge. Openings in the forest provide stunning views of Mount Hood, with a high ridge of Yocum Ridge to the right, and the valley of the Muddy Fork of the Sandy River far below. Wildflowers in the alpine meadows include red paintbrush, blue lupine, avalanche lilies, western pasqueflower, beargrass, heather, and pink spiraea.

At a scenic alpine area with tarns (ponds created by snow melt), stay right at all junctions, hiking through forest, past rock slides and up a ridge beside Ladd Creek. At times, the trail is hard to distinguish, going through thick shrubbery. Just past timberline, snowfields can linger on the rocky slopes all year. Cross the snowfields and continue to the McNeil Point stone shelter, built in the 1930s by the Civilian Conservation Corps.

Take in amazing views in all directions, including Mount Rainier, Mount St. Helens and Mount Adams. For a closer look at the Sandy and Glisan glaciers, continue on the trail above the shelter for a few hundred feet. After soaking in this glorious high mountain region, return the same way.

Conditions on this high exposed area can change quickly, so be prepared with warm layers of clothing and rain gear. A good general rule is that if the mountain is completely socked in, it's best to do this hike another day. It's easy to get lost in high mountain terrain, and the effort to get there is better rewarded when there are views all around.

Distance: 9.6 miles (roundtrip)

Elevation Gain: 2,220 ft.

Difficulty: difficult

Hike type: out and back

Trail: packed dirt and rock

Typical open: mid-July - mid-Oct.

Best time of year: Aug. - Oct.

Features: forest, alpine meadows, mountain views, glaciers

Fees/permits: Northwest Forest Pass required

Agency: Hood River Ranger District, Mount Hood National Forest (see pg. 126)

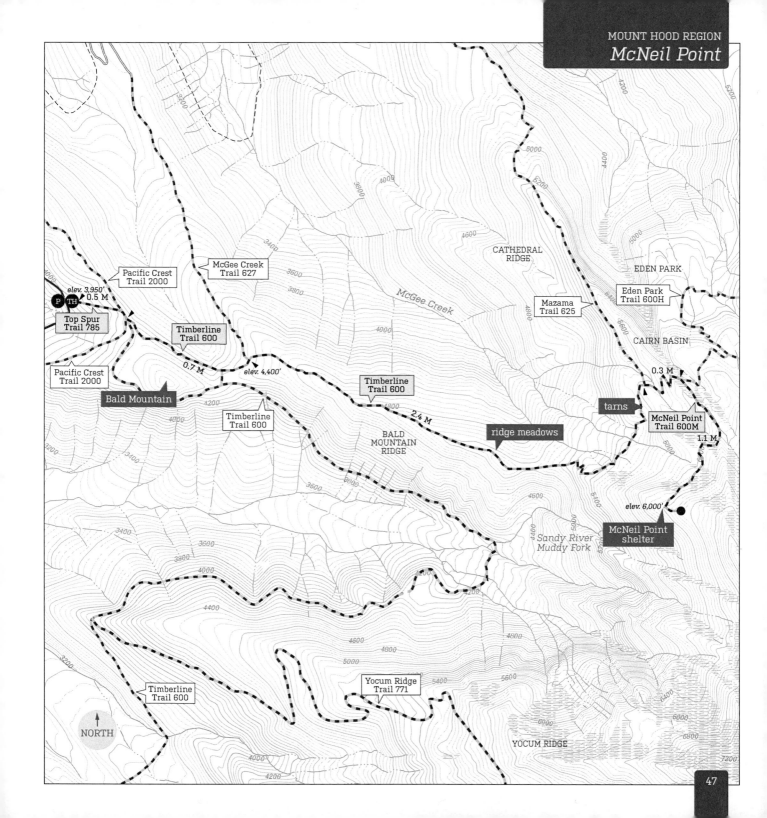

Pacific Crest
Trail 2000

McGee Creek
Trail 627

elev. 3,950'
0.5 M

Top Spur
Trail 785

Timberline
Trail 600

Pacific Crest
Trail 2000

0.7 M

elev. 4,400'

Bald Mountain

Timberline
Trail 600

McGee Creek

CATHEDRAL
RIDGE

EDEN PARK

Eden Park
Trail 600H

Mazama
Trail 625

CAIRN BASIN

0.3 M

Timberline
Trail 600

2.4 M

BALD
MOUNTAIN
RIDGE

ridge meadows

tarns

McNeil Point
Trail 600M

1.1 M

elev. 6,000'

Sandy River
Muddy Fork

McNeil Point
shelter

Timberline
Trail 600

Yocum Ridge
Trail 771

NORTH

YOCUM RIDGE

Hike along the Sandy River glacial floodplain to magnificent Ramona Falls. Return along scenic Ramona Creek as it meanders through a mossy forest.

DIRECTIONS

From Portland: drive 42 miles east on U.S. 26 to Zigzag.

Across from the Zigzag Ranger District, turn left onto East Lolo Pass Road.

Continue on Lolo Pass Road for 4.2 miles, then turn right on paved Forest Road 1825.

Drive for 0.7 miles on Forest Road 1825 and turn right to cross the Sandy River on a bridge.

Continue for another 1.7 miles and bear left at the junction onto Forest Road 1825-100.

Continue for 0.5 miles to a large parking lot.

Drive time from Portland: 1 hour 25 minutes

THE HIKE

One of the most popular hikes on the west side of Mount Hood, the trailhead is in the Sandy River floodplain – a sandy, rocky, and desolate area due to the glacial fed river that runs through this valley. The milky color of the river is due to the silt it carries, which starts as rock on Mount Hood that gets worn down by the glaciers.

From the trailhead, take the Sandy River Trail one mile to a temporary bridge over the river. This bridge is removed every fall and put back in mid-spring by the Forest Service. If the bridge isn't in place, this can be a very difficult and dangerous water crossing, with water levels rising significantly later in the day due to snow melt. *UPDATE: the seasonal bridge washed away in a rainstorm and will not be replaced, so fording the Sandy River is now required for this hike.*

Just after the bridge, the trail is sometimes hard to follow. Look for signs of the trail indicated by small rocks and tree branches placed to help show where to go. The only views of Mount Hood are in this short section, so stop to take it in if the mountain isn't hiding behind clouds.

In about .25 miles, the loop trail begins at a trail junction. Since either direction is about the same distance to the falls, you can choose which section of this starkly contrasting loop to do first. The trail to the right follows the Sandy River and looks much like the trail you've taken so far. This portion of the trail is open to equestrians, and provides access to a backpackers' camp south of the waterfall. The more scenic trail to the left follows Ramona Creek as it meanders through a mossy forest. The sheer rock walls of Yocum Ridge are visible through the trees for a portion of this section. Both trails travel through a forest of lodgepole pine, mountain hemlock, and Douglas fir.

No matter which direction you choose, Ramona Falls (120 ft.) is the highlight of this hike. Appearing to come from nowhere, the waterfall fans out and cascades down a large wall of columnar basalt. The area around the falls can get crowded, but there are plenty of spots to spread out and enjoy the wonder of the falls. Either return the same way you came, or continue on the loop shown on the map.

Distance: 7 miles (roundtrip)

Elevation Gain: 1,100 ft.

Difficulty: moderate

Hike type: loop

Trail: rock, sand, packed dirt

Typical open: May - Oct., depending on snow levels

Best time of year: June - Sept.

Features: waterfall, forest, creeks

Fees/permits: Northwest Forest Pass required

Agency: Zig Zag Ranger District, Mount Hood National Forest (see pg. 126)

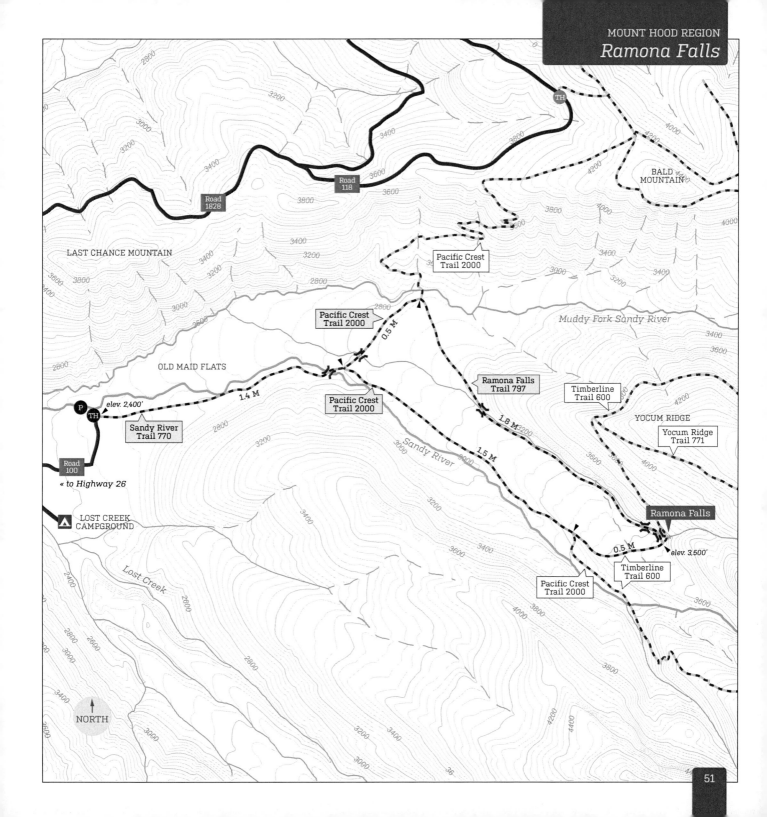

2800

3200

3400

3000

3200

3400

3800

3600

3400

Road
1828

Road
118

3600

TH

4000

4200

BALD
MOUNTAIN

3800

4000

4200

4000

LAST CHANCE MOUNTAIN

3400

3200

3600

3800

3400

2800

3000

3600

2800

Pacific Crest
Trail 2000

3000

3400

Muddy Fork Sandy River

3400

3600

OLD MAID FLATS

Pacific Crest
Trail 2000

2800

0.5 M

1.4 M

P
TH

elev. 2,400'

Sandy River
Trail 770

Pacific Crest
Trail 2000

Ramona Falls
Trail 797

Timberline
Trail 600

4200

YOCUM RIDGE

Yocum Ridge
Trail 771

1.8 M

3200

Road
100

2800

3200

Sandy River

1.5 M

3000

3600

4000

« to Highway 26

LOST CREEK
CAMPGROUND

3400

3200

Ramona Falls

0.5 M

elev. 3,500'

Timberline
Trail 600

Lost Creek

3600

3400

Pacific Crest
Trail 2000

4000

3800

2400

2600

2800

3000

3600

3600

3200

3400

4200

4400

3800

NORTH

3000

3000

36

Salmon River Canyon ⑨

Hike beside the Salmon River through a mossy forest with old-growth cedar and fir, primitive campsites, and spring wildflowers to a canyon viewpoint above the river.

DIRECTIONS

From Portland, drive east on Highway 26 for 40 miles to the town of Welches.

One mile past the Welches shopping center, turn right on Salmon River Road.

Continue on the Salmon River Road for five miles, passing several trailheads for the Old Salmon River Trail.

Trailhead parking is on both sides of the road, just before a bridge crossing the Salmon River.

Drive time from Portland: 1 hour 15 minutes

THE HIKE

The Salmon River is a designated Wild and Scenic River, all the way from its beginnings at the Palmer snowfield on Mount Hood to where it joins the Sandy River near Brightwood 33 miles later.

Begin this hike at the trailhead located right before a bridge going over the Salmon River. The first two miles of the hike are relatively flat, skirting above the river bank several times, and meandering through an old-growth forest of Douglas fir, western red cedar, and western hemlock. Fallen trees become "nurse" logs, giving life to the moss, ferns, and young trees growing from them. Moss and lichens hang from the trees and cover interesting rocky structures. In late April and early May, spring wildflowers are abundant, including fawn lilies, oxalis, chocolate lilies, yellow violets and fairy slippers. The forest floor is covered with oxalis, changing to Oregon grape and salal as you climb up before reaching a rocky meadow.

Along the way, you'll cross two sturdy footbridges made of stripped logs, the second crossing a picturesque creek that cascades over mossy rocks before meeting the Salmon River. About 1.5 miles in is Rolling Riffle Camp, a small area of rustic camping spots between the trail and the river. A checkpoint for the Salmon-Huckleberry Wilderness is about 2 miles in. Shortly after, the trail begins to climb, sometimes steeply, and swings in away from the river several times to cross several small drainage areas.

Once you climb out of the forested section, bear to the right and stay on the narrow, rocky trail to a spectacular canyon overlook. The river is about 600 feet below, and you can hear the roar of several unseen waterfalls. There are steep scramble paths below, but the rocky slopes are very slippery, and people have fallen off and died while attempting this, so stay on the main trail. Look for wildflowers in this exposed rocky area, including Indian paintbrush. After the canyon overlook, the trail is much steeper, so this is a good place to turn around and head back the same way.

Distance: 7.2 miles (roundtrip)

Elevation Gain: 950 ft.

Difficulty: moderate

Hike type: out and back

Trail: packed dirt

Typical open: all year, depending on snow levels

Best time of year: May - Sept.

Features: river, forest, canyon views, wildflowers

Fees/permits: Northwest Forest Pass required

Agency: Zig Zag Ranger District, Mount Hood National Forest (see pg. 126)

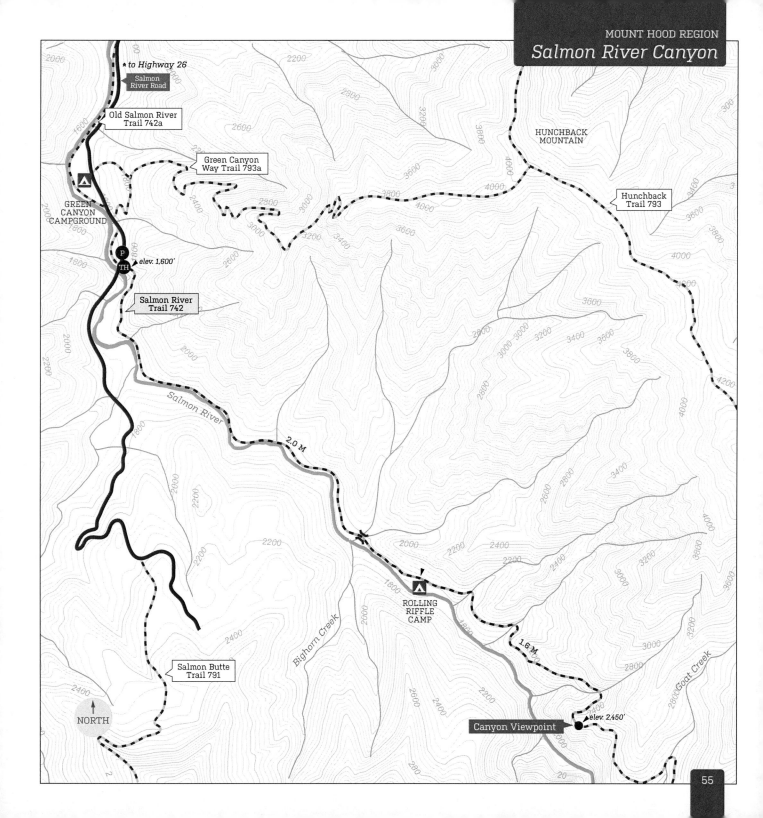

to Highway 26

Salmon River Road

Old Salmon River Trail 742a

Green Canyon Way Trail 793a

HUNCHBACK MOUNTAIN

Hunchback Trail 793

GREEN CANYON CAMPGROUND

P

TH

elev. 1,600'

Salmon River Trail 742

Salmon River

2.0 M

Bighorn Creek

Goat Creek

ROLLING RIFFLE CAMP

1.6 M

Salmon Butte Trail 791

NORTH

Canyon Viewpoint

elev. 2,450'

Twin Lakes Snowshoe

10

Leave behind the heavy crowds at other Mount Hood winter destinations on this forested snowshoe hike to a small mountain lake.

DIRECTIONS

From Portland, drive east on Highway 26 for 45 miles to the Frog Lake Sno-Park at Wapinitia Pass, located 7 miles southeast of Government Camp and 4 miles south of the Hwy. 26/35 junction.

Park near the north end of the parking lot. The trailhead is to the left of the vault toilets.

Drive time from Portland: 1 hour 40 minutes

THE HIKE

Snowshoeing is just like hiking, only with snowshoes on your feet in addition to your boots, so a slightly wider stance is needed when hiking. Otherwise, it's an easy way to enjoy the beauty of winter in the mountains without needing a lot of gear or the risks of downhill skiing. Good snow conditions for snowshoeing in this area are when there is at least 3-5 feet of snow on the ground, preferably just after recent snowfall so the trail isn't a hard-pack of icy snow.

Outfitting for a snowshoe hike in the winter includes a base layer of wool or synthetic material for moisture wicking insulation (cotton is not a good choice since it stays wet and pulls heat from your body instead of insulating it), a middle layer for warmth, and a top waterproof layer including rain pants and waterproof jacket. The key is to wear layers so it is easy to make adjustments as needed to stay warm or cool off.

Trekking poles outfitted with a snow basket are helpful for keeping your balance and crossing any difficult terrain. One additional tip for snowshoeing: it's much easier to step forward on snowshoes than it is to step backwards, so to avoid falling, move forward in a circle to turn around.

Look for the Twin Lakes trailhead at the north end of the parking lot near the restroom. Snowmobilers aren't allowed on this trail and will instead be using the Frog Lake trail at the south end of the parking lot.

After a very short distance on this trail connector, turn right on the Pacific Crest Trail #2000. The forest is full of towering mountain hemlocks with snow clinging to the sprays of branches. Climb gradually for a half mile to a sharp turn in the trail. Continue north for another mile to a junction with the Twin Lakes trail. Turn right and head downhill along a ridge slope to the small mountain lake basin that holds Lower Twin Lake. An open area in the woods beside the lake makes for a nice spot to take a break before heading back the same way. It's common for birds to dip and pick up any stray tidbits of food you drop, so don't be alarmed if a fast swooping bird buzzes right by. Return the same way.

Distance: 4.2 miles (roundtrip)

Elevation Gain: 700 ft.

Difficulty: easy to moderate

Hike type: out and back

Trail: snow in winter

Typical open: Oct. - April, but check on snow conditions first

Best time of year: Dec. - Feb.

Features: snow, forest, lake

Fees/permits: Oregon Sno-Park permit required Nov. 1 through April 30

Agency: Hood River Ranger District, Mount Hood National Forest (see pg. 126)

58

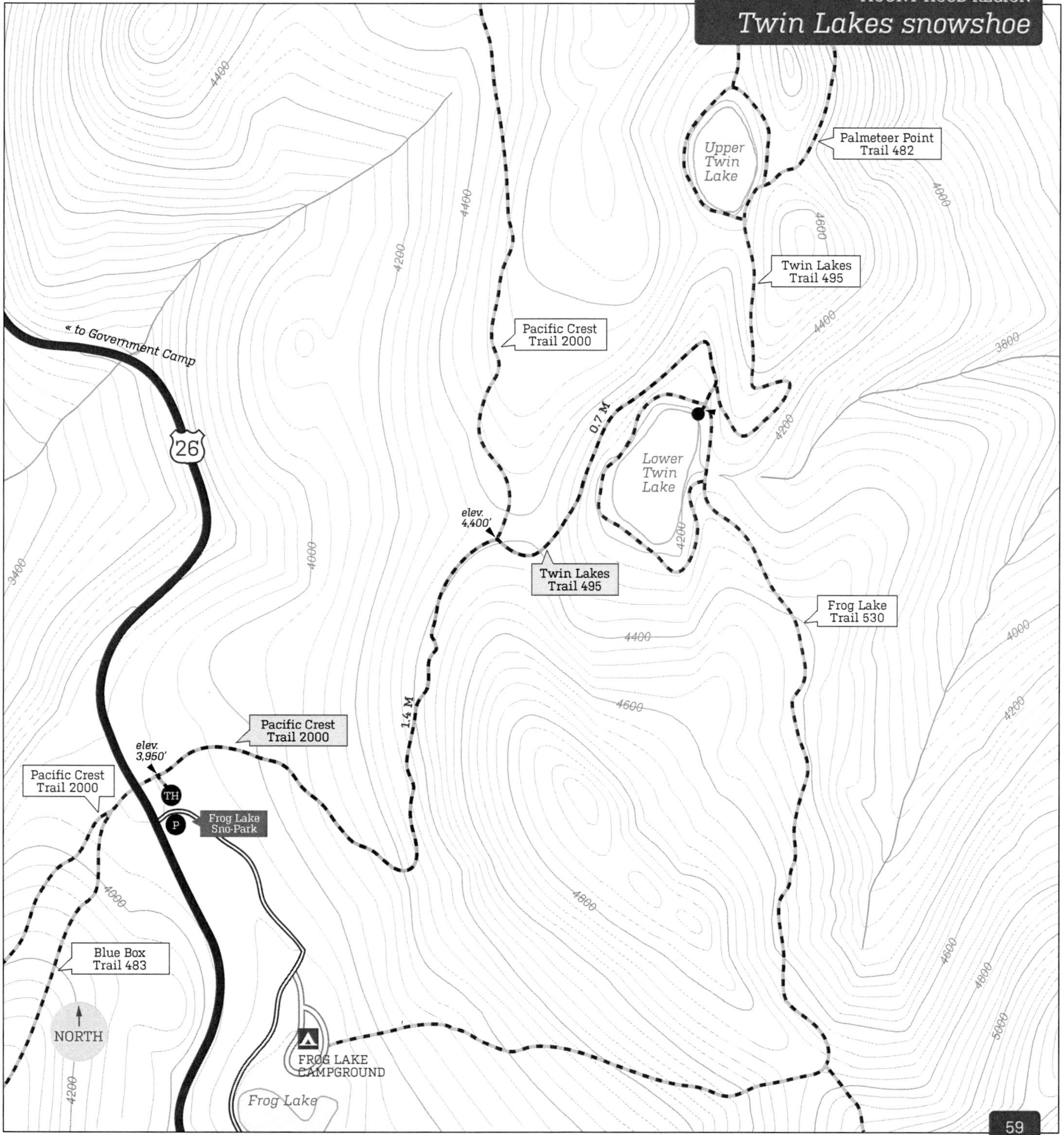

Upper Twin Lake
Palmeteer Point Trail 482
Twin Lakes Trail 495
Pacific Crest Trail 2000
« to Government Camp
26
0.7 M
Lower Twin Lake
elev. 4,400'
Twin Lakes Trail 495
Frog Lake Trail 530
1.4 M
Pacific Crest Trail 2000
elev. 3,950'
Pacific Crest Trail 2000
TH
P
Frog Lake Sno-Park
Blue Box Trail 483
NORTH
FROG LAKE CAMPGROUND
Frog Lake
4400
4200
4000
3800
3400
4600
4800
5000

Tom Dick & Harry Mountain

11

Located next to Mount Hood, this hike to Mirror Lake and the rocky summit of Tom Dick and Harry Mountain has great views of the Cascades.

DIRECTIONS

From Portland, drive east on Highway 26 for 51 miles to the Mirror Lake trailhead, between mileposts 51 and 52 and one-half mile past the historic marker for Laurel Hill Chute.

Drive time from Portland: 1 hour 15 minutes

THE HIKE

The portion of this hike that goes to Mirror Lake is extremely popular in the summer, especially for families with children, and the parking area fills up quickly, so go early on weekends, or plan a mid-week trip.

Cross a small bridge over Camp Creek just upstream from unseen Yocum Falls and enter a mixed evergreen forest of Douglas fir, white pine, western hemlock and western red cedar, with rhododendrons and vine maples in the understory. The rhododendrons usually bloom in June.

The trail is well-graded and wide, with switchbacks up the gradual ascent to Mirror Lake, a small mountain lake that is a classic glacial cirque – a feature formed by water filling in a circular basin carved by glaciers. Crossing a large rock slide, stop quietly and you may see pikas – small mammals related to rabbits with rounded ears, no visible tail, and a high-pitched, squeaky call.

After several additional switchbacks, reach the Mirror Lake trail junction. Choose to loop around the lake, or continue straight to the shoreline of the lake. A great view of Mount Hood with the lake in the foreground is along the loop trail on a marshy section with boardwalk.

Just past the lake, the trail continues to the summit of the Harry ridge of Tom Dick and Harry Mountain, named for the three ridges on the mountain. The trail here is steeper, with two mile-long traverses. There are multiple views of Mount Hood and the surrounding valleys in open areas along the trail, with beargrass, pink spiraea, Indian paintbrush and other wildflowers during the summer.

A large cairn – a man-made stack of rocks – is just before the point where the trail turns to the left. Wild huckleberry shrubs line the path, ripening in August for a tasty treat. The last one-third mile climbs more steeply on rocky terrain before reaching the base of the summit. The approach to the rock-capped summit is a light scramble up boulders. At the top, take in the stellar views of Mount Hood right before you, and several other snow-capped peaks along the horizon, including Mount St. Helens, Mount Adams and Mount Jefferson. Mount Rainier may also be visible directly behind Mount St. Helens. Return the same way.

Distance: 6.4 miles (roundtrip)

Elevation Gain: 1,500 ft.

Difficulty: moderate

Hike type: out and back

Trail: packed dirt

Typical open: June - Oct., depending on snow levels

Best time of year: June - Aug.

Features: forest, lake, mountain views

Fees/permits: Northwest Forest Pass required

Agency: Zig Zag Ranger District, Mount Hood National Forest (see pg. 126)

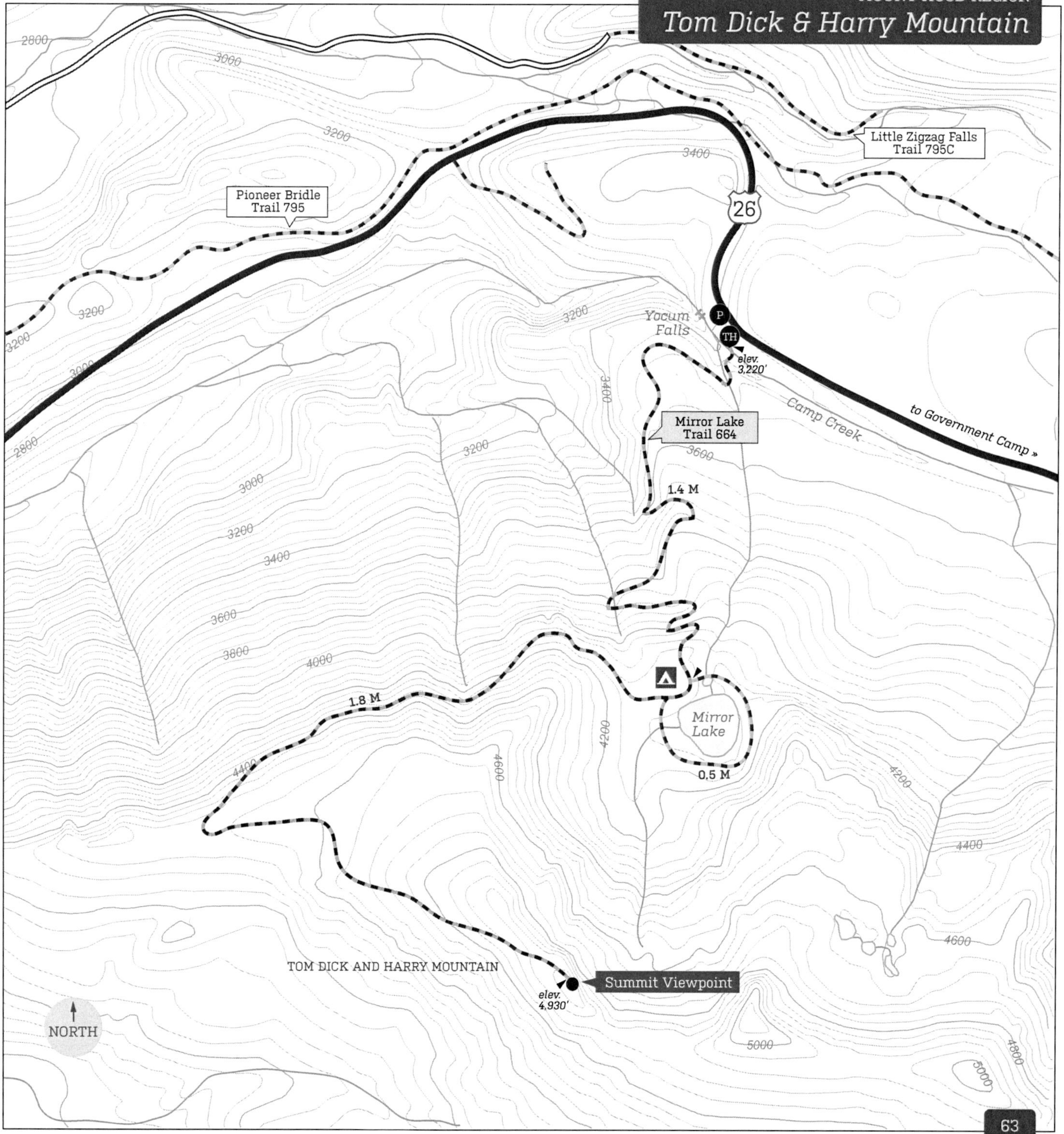

Little Zigzag Falls
Trail 795C
Pioneer Bridle
Trail 795
26
Yocum
Falls
P
TH
elev.
3,220'
Camp Creek
to Government Camp »
Mirror Lake
Trail 664
1.4 M
Mirror
Lake
0.5 M
1.8 M
TOM DICK AND HARRY MOUNTAIN
Summit Viewpoint
elev.
4,930'
NORTH
2800
3000
3200
3400
3600
3800
4000
4200
4400
4600
4800
5000

Tamanawas Falls

12

The only views of Mount Hood for this hike are on the drive to the trailhead. Instead, come here for the beauty of the mossy green Cold Spring Creek canyon and 100 ft. tall Tamanawas Falls.

DIRECTIONS

From Portland, drive east on I-84 for 62 miles to Hood River.

Take exit 64 for Highway 35.

Travel south on Hwy. 35 for 25 miles to the Polallie picnic area and Elk Meadows trailhead.

Drive time from Portland: 1 hour 30 minutes

THE HIKE

A Native American word, Tamanawas means "friendly spirit guide." It's not hard to imagine friendly spirits enjoying the breathtaking scenery here.

Most people begin at the East Fork trailhead for a shorter hike, but for a longer, much less crowded hike, begin at the Elk Meadows trailhead to the north, parking at the Polallie picnic area. The trailhead is not well marked, but is easy to find. Look directly across the highway from the parking lot for a trail heading uphill.

For the first 1.5 miles, travel through heavy forest with a mix of western red cedar and Douglas fir. Occasionally, the forest opens enough to catch a peek of Mount Adams to the north. After 1.3 miles is a trail junction with the Tamanawas Falls Tie Trail (#650B). Turn here and descend for just over .25 miles to a junction with the Tamanawas Trail (#650A). Turn right and pass through an area filled with extra large boulders, following the trail to Tamanawas Falls (100 ft.). Traversing across a steep talus slope, it is possible to reach a small amphitheater behind the falls.

From the falls, return to the junction and stay on the Tamanawas Falls Trail as it meanders along Cold Spring Creek, a tributary of the East Fork Hood River. This section of the hike is the prettiest, with plenty of spots to access the mossy banks of the creek. For the return loop to Polallie trailhead, turn left at a junction just uphill from a rustic bridge crossing the creek. This section of trail traverses up and down the hillside several times parallel to the highway, although it is far enough above it to feel somewhat secluded. There are a couple of small creek crossings, and waterproof boots will be handy during higher water levels.

For a shorter hike, park at the East Fork trailhead located about a mile south of the Polallie picnic area. From here, it's just over half a mile to the Tamanawas Trail, and includes a newer footbridge over the raging waters of the East Fork Hood River.

Distance: 4.2 miles (roundtrip)

Elevation Gain: 900 ft.

Difficulty: moderate

Hike type: loop

Trail: packed dirt and rock

Typical open: May - Nov., depending on snow levels

Best time of year: June - Oct.

Features: waterfall, creek, forest

Fees/permits: Northwest Forest Pass required

Agency: Hood River Ranger District, Mount Hood National Forest (see pg. 126)

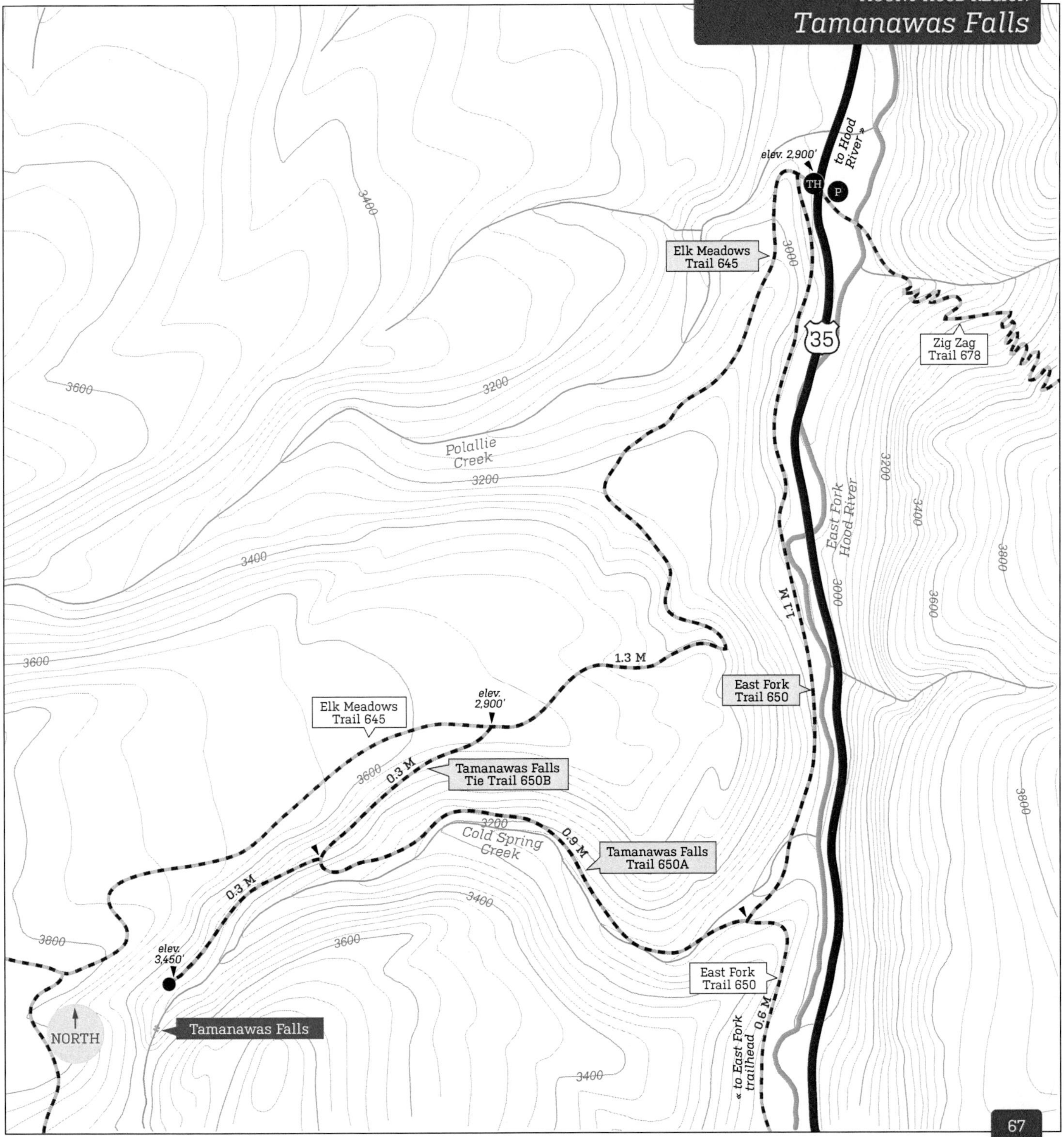

3400

3600

3200

Polallie
Creek

3200

3400

3600

elev. 2,900'

TH P

to Hood River

Elk Meadows
Trail 645

US 35

Zig Zag
Trail 678

3200

3400

3600

3800

East Fork
Hood River

3000

1.1 M

1.3 M

elev.
2,900'

Elk Meadows
Trail 645

3600

0.3 M

Tamanawas Falls
Tie Trail 650B

East Fork
Trail 650

3200

Cold Spring
Creek

0.9 M

Tamanawas Falls
Trail 650A

3800

0.3 M

3400

3600

3800

elev.
3,450'

NORTH

Tamanawas Falls

East Fork
Trail 650

« to East Fork
trailhead

0.6 M

3400

Lost Lake Butte

Hike to the top of a butte with expansive views of Mount Hood and other Cascade mountains, then walk among old-growth cedar on a boardwalk trail, or do a loop around Lost Lake with its postcard-worthy views of Mount Hood.

DIRECTIONS

From Portland, drive east on I-84 to Hood River and take exit 62.

Turn right on Cascade Ave. (Highway 30) and continue for about a mile.

Turn right on 13th St. and then right on 12th St.

12th St. becomes Tucker, which you will stay on (despite it turning right and left) until Tucker becomes Dee Hood River Highway.

Take the Dee Highway 6.5 miles to Dee, and exit Lost Lake Road.

Follow Lost Lake Road through Dee.

Continue on Lost Lake Road, which becomes Forest Road 13.

Park next to a gated spur road with a sign marking the Skyline Trail 655, just before the campground entry booth.

Drive time from Portland: 2 hours

THE HIKE

An incredibly scenic mountain lake with outstanding views of Mount Hood, Lost Lake has a large campground (privately managed) with a general store, non-motorized boat rentals, and several trails for hiking and exploring.

To find the trailhead: if you are parked at the Old Skyline spur road just before the campground entry, take the Skyline Trail for .3 mile to a signed junction with the Lost Lake Butte trailhead. If you parked in the day use area, follow a path through the campground uphill to the signed trailhead between the C loop and the walk-in sites in the E loop.

The hike to the top of Lost Lake Butte climbs at a moderate ascent, at times steeply, to gain 1,300 ft. in just over 2 miles. The forest is filled with an understory of beargrass and rhododendrons. A member of the lily family, beargrass was long used by Native Americans to weave into baskets. Blooming only once every 5-7 years in late spring and early summer, each plant can reach 5 feet tall with large cream-colored blooms.

The last .75 miles of trail is a series of eight switchbacks. An old fire lookout that was destroyed in the 1960s is just below the summit. Stay to the right and continue on the trail as it goes through a thicket of trees and shrubs at the summit. An open area with large boulders provides a panoramic view of Mount Hood, with distant views of Mount St. Helens, Mount Adams, Mount Jefferson and Mount Rainier. Lost Lake is below to the south, but trees at the summit block the view. Return the same way.

Optional trails: back at the campground, a boardwalk meanders for .75 miles through a grove of old-growth cedar. Interpretive signs along the trail provide ecology highlights. The trailhead is near the day use parking area, west of the campground loop road. The lakeshore trail loops the perimeter of Lost Lake for an easy 3.2 mile walk. Catch a spectacular view of Mount Hood from the north end of the lake.

Distance: 4.6 miles (roundtrip)

Elevation Gain: 1,300 ft.

Difficulty: moderate

Hike type: out and back

Trail: packed dirt

Typical open: June - Oct., depending on snow levels

Best time of year: July - Sept.

Features: lake, old-growth forest, mountain views

Fees/permits: The lake is privately managed and requires a $6 day fee (per car) for parking at the day use area. Otherwise, park at the Old Skyline trailhead (no fee required).

Agency: Hood River Ranger District, Mount Hood National Forest (see pg. 126)

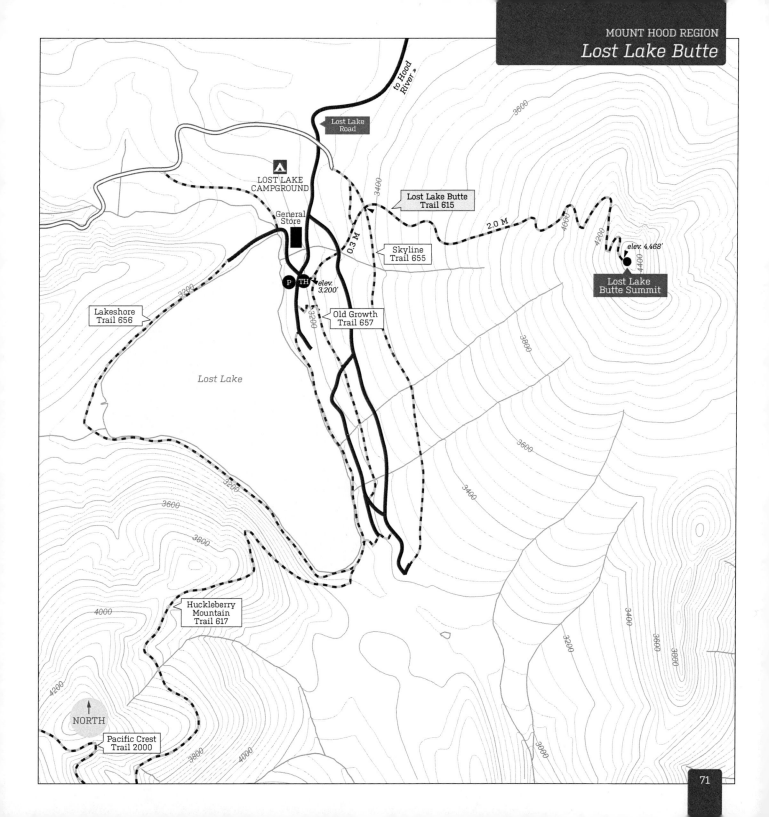

Lost Lake
Road

to Hood River »

LOST LAKE
CAMPGROUND

Lost Lake Butte
Trail 615

2.0 M

elev. 4,468'

Lost Lake
Butte Summit

General
Store

Skyline
Trail 655

0.3 M

P TH *elev. 3,200'*

Lakeshore
Trail 656

Old Growth
Trail 657

Lost Lake

3200

3600

3800

4000

Huckleberry
Mountain
Trail 617

4200

NORTH

Pacific Crest
Trail 2000

3800

4000

3000

3200

3400

3600

3800

4000

4200

4400

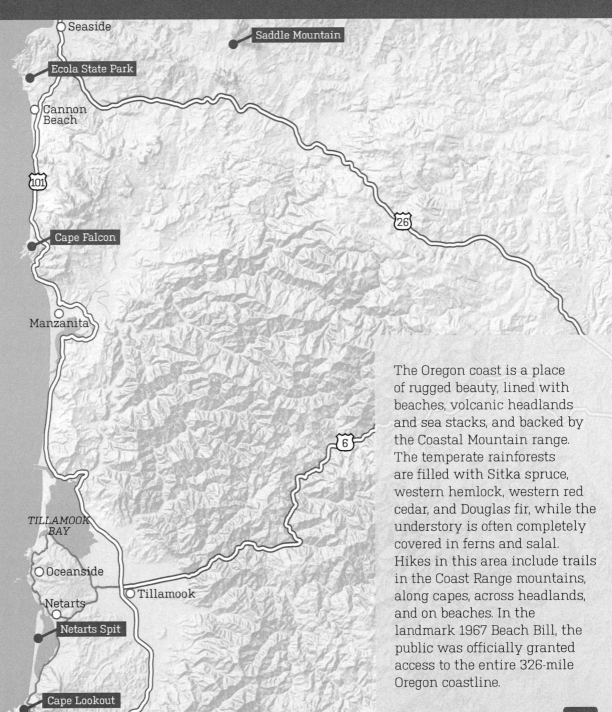

Oregon Coast

Seaside

Saddle Mountain

Ecola State Park

Cannon
Beach

101

Cape Falcon

Manzanita

PACIFIC OCEAN

26

6

TILLAMOOK
BAY

Oceanside

Netarts

Tillamook

Netarts Spit

Cape Lookout

The Oregon coast is a place
of rugged beauty, lined with
beaches, volcanic headlands
and sea stacks, and backed by
the Coastal Mountain range.
The temperate rainforests
are filled with Sitka spruce,
western hemlock, western red
cedar, and Douglas fir, while the
understory is often completely
covered in ferns and salal.
Hikes in this area include trails
in the Coast Range mountains,
along capes, across headlands,
and on beaches. In the
landmark 1967 Beach Bill, the
public was officially granted
access to the entire 326-mile
Oregon coastline.

Located in Oregon's Coast Range mountains, this is a strenuous hike up steep terrain with spectacular wildflower-covered slopes in the spring and a 360-degree view at the summit.

DIRECTIONS

From Portland, drive 63 miles west on Highway 26 to the Saddle Mountain State Park Road.

Continue for 7 miles to the Saddle Mountain State Park parking lot.

Drive time from Portland: 1 hour 30 minutes

THE HIKE

Best hiked during clear days in late spring to early summer, this challenging hike offers great rewards for the effort.

Saddle Mountain (3,283 ft.) was formed when this area was all part of the ocean. The prominent top portions of the "saddle" are pillow basalt, formed about 15 million years ago when the lava flows of the Columbia River basalt floods were quickly cooled by sea water.

The trail to the top is steep and difficult in spots, with chain link fence material covering loose rocky portions of the trail. The wire provides better traction, but it also sometimes requires walking at sharp angles that quickly tire feet and calves. Heavy wire cable strung between metal posts provides hand rails along some sections of trail.

Begin the hike at the trailhead near the small 10-site campground through an alder, Douglas fir, and red maple forest with a thick salmonberry understory that creates a tunnel-like feel. After 0.2 miles, take the Humbug Mountain side trail to great views of both Humbug and Saddle Mountains. The dense forest is scenic in this section, with a carpet of green oxalis covering the ground.

The trail soon begins switchbacks up through a forest of hemlock and spruce, with openings providing views of the surrounding Coast Range and valley. At about 1.5 miles in, the trail traverses grassy open meadows filled with more than 300 types of wildflowers, some of which are quite rare. Look for an ancient basalt dike that resembles a rock wall descending down the mountain's slopes in this section.

After a short descent through the saddle area, the final climb up to the summit is visible. The site of a former lookout tower, the top is open and rocky with railings on all sides. On a clear day, the views range from the Pacific ocean and the Columbia River to Cascade peaks, including Mount Rainier, Mount St. Helens, Mount Hood, and Mount Jefferson. Return the same way.

Weather conditions can change rapidly, so bring wind and rain gear year round and ice or snow gear in winter.

Distance: 5.6 miles (roundtrip)

Elevation Gain: 1,700 ft.

Difficulty: difficult

Hike type: out and back

Trail: packed dirt and rock

Typical open: March - June

Best time of year: May - June

Features: views, wildflowers, coastal forest

Fees/permits: none

Agency: Saddle Mountain State Park, Oregon State Parks (see pg. 126)

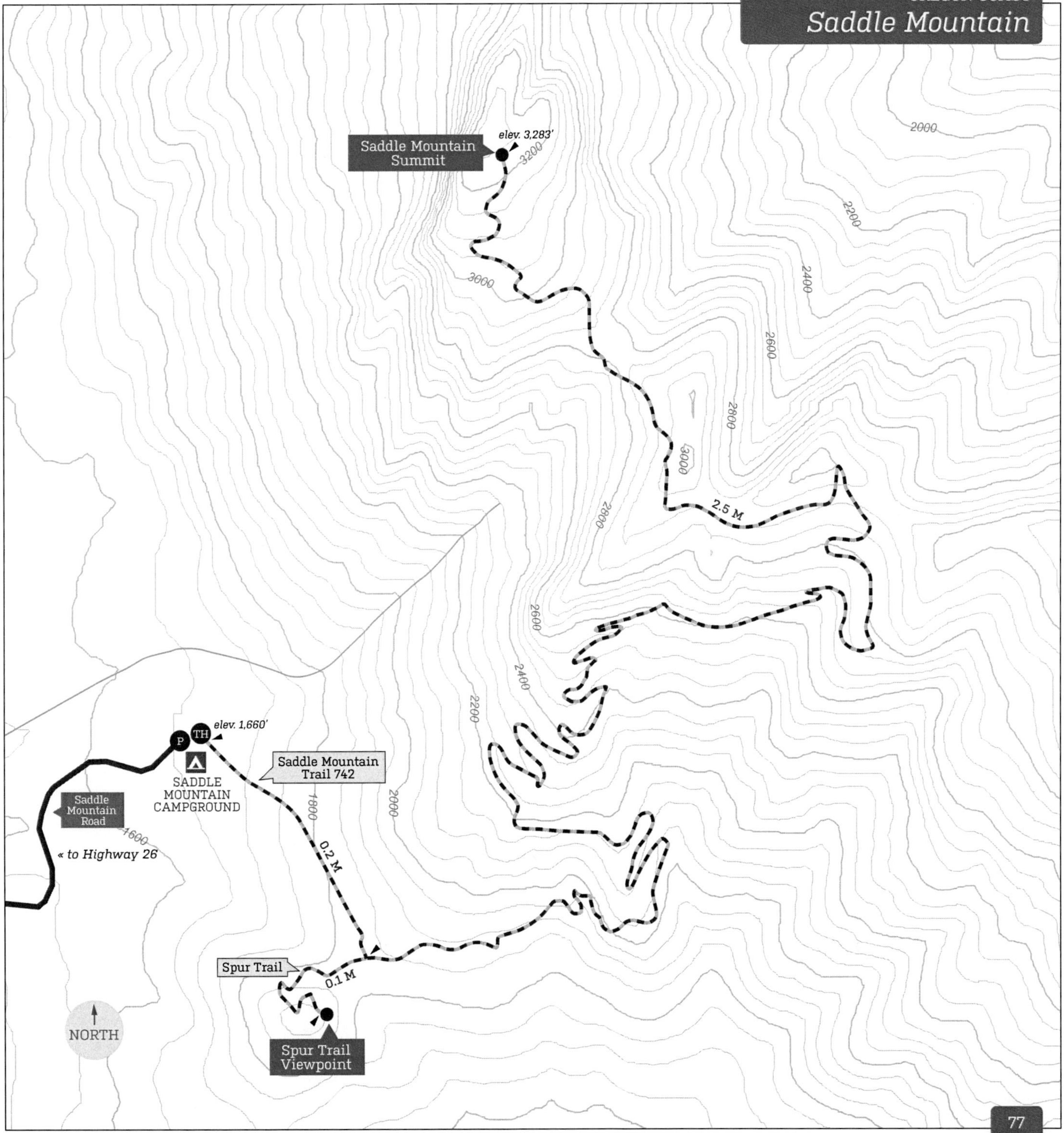

Saddle Mountain
Summit

elev. 3,283'

2000

2200

2400

2600

2800

3000

2.5 M

3600

3200

3000

2800

2600

2400

2200

2000

1800

elev. 1,660'

P   TH

SADDLE
MOUNTAIN
CAMPGROUND

Saddle Mountain
Trail 742

Saddle
Mountain
Road

« to Highway 26

1600

0.2 M

Spur Trail

0.1 M

Spur Trail
Viewpoint

NORTH

Cape Falcon + Short Sand Beach

Combine a short hike through old-growth coastal rainforest to the tip of a scenic cape with a side trip to secluded but busy Short Sand Beach, a popular destination for surfers.

DIRECTIONS

From Portland, drive 74 miles west on Highway 26.

Take the US 101 South exit (Oregon Coast Highway).

Continue for 14 miles and park in the northernmost (on the right side of the highway) of the park's three parking areas.

Drive time from Portland: 1 hour 45 minutes

THE HIKE

Begin the hike at the parking area trailhead marked for Cape Falcon. The trail runs along the side of a forested ridge above Short Sand Creek for a half mile to a junction. To visit Short Sand Beach, turn left. For the Cape Falcon hike, turn right and follow the trail towards the cape.

The campground here was closed in 2009 after a large tree fell on the camp sites. Foresters determined that up to 50 more old-growth trees were susceptible to falling, so with public input, it was decided to close the campground instead of removing the ancient trees.

Beginning in a forest of Sitka spruce, western hemlock, western red cedar, and fir and filled with ferns, the trail goes through wet boggy areas that are usually quite muddy. Frequent coastal storms mean that there can be lots of blowdown on the trail too, so climbing around fallen trees and washed out trail is common. In early spring, trilliums and skunk cabbage are seen (and smelled).

As the trail climbs the cape, ocean waves crash below and the forest opens to provide views of the beach. The trail soon descends and crosses a small creek. Look for a side trail on the left that goes to a viewpoint of Blumenthal Falls.

Continue on the main trail along several switchbacks going up to the headland. Native salal on both sides of the trail form a high tunnel as you make your way along an often muddy trench between them.

At the top of the headland, take the left spur where the trail divides. There are several open areas along the cliff edge to take in the views all around. To reach the end of the cape, look for an obvious but unsigned trail heading into a shrubby knoll. Work your way through the vegetation to the narrow and rocky cape. Be careful to not get too close to the sheer edges of the cape here. The view to the south includes Neahkahnie Mountain and the beach town of Manzanita, and on clear days, views to the north all the way to Tillamook Head and south to Cape Lookout. Return the same way.

Distance: 5 miles (roundtrip)

Elevation Gain: 260 ft.

Difficulty: easy

Hike type: out and back

Trail: packed dirt

Typical open: all year

Best time of year: all year, except during winter storms

Features: coastal forest, beach, ocean views, whale watching

Fees/permits: none

Agency: Oswald West State Park, Oregon State Parks (see pg. 126)

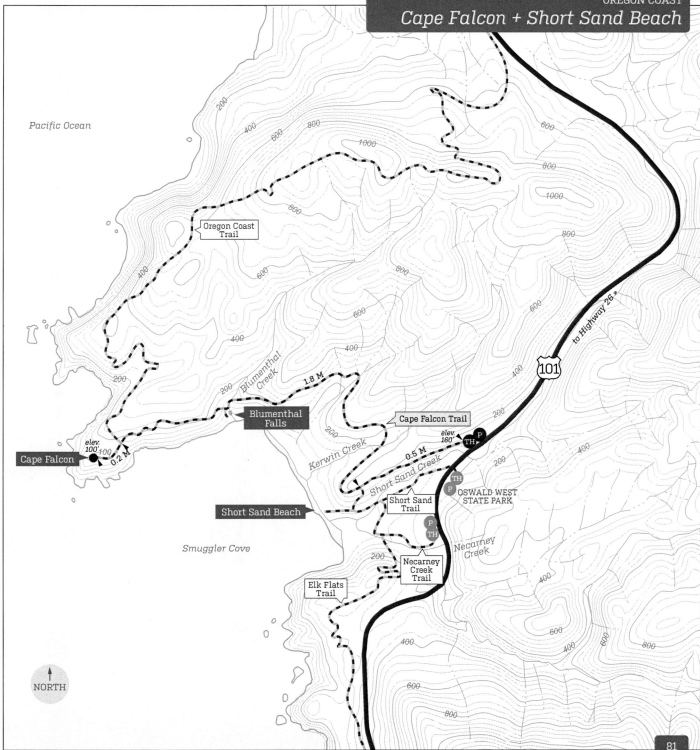

Pacific Ocean

Oregon Coast Trail

1000

800

600

400

200

to Highway 26 »

101

Blumenthal Creek

1.8 M

Blumenthal Falls

Cape Falcon Trail

elev. 160'

TH   P

0.5 M

Short Sand Creek

Kerwin Creek

Cape Falcon

elev. 100'

100

0.2 M

Short Sand Trail

TH
P

OSWALD WEST STATE PARK

Short Sand Beach

Smuggler Cove

P
TH

Necarney Creek

Necarney Creek Trail

Elk Flats Trail

NORTH

Cape Lookout juts two miles into the Pacific Ocean on a slender promontory of basalt headland with old-growth coastal rainforest and spectacular views 400 feet above the ocean.

DIRECTIONS

From Portland, drive west for 20 miles on Highway 26 to the Highway 6 exit.

Stay to the left and continue on Highway 6 for 50 miles through the Coast Range to Tillamook.

At the Highway 101 junction in Tillamook, follow signs for Cape Lookout State Park, continuing straight on 1st St.

Turn left on Birch St., then right on 3rd St., which becomes Netarts Highway.

Continue on Netarts Highway for 4.5 miles.

Following signs for Cape Lookout State Park, turn left at Whiskey Creek Road.

Continue for about 8 miles, passing the park entrance, to the trailhead parking lot at the top of a hill on the right..

Drive time from Portland: 1 hour 45 minutes

THE HIKE

Cape Lookout was formed 15 million years ago when massive lava floods flowed down the Columbia River and fanned out down the coastline, hardening into basalt headlands.

At the trailhead, take the Cape Trail, heading straight along this 2 mile cape that juts westward into the Pacific ocean. Since this part of the Oregon coast receives about 100 inches of rain each year, the trail is often wet and mucky, so plan on getting your boots or shoes muddy. There are short sections of boardwalks along the trail, but there are plenty of spots where the mud covers the entire trail without the boardwalks.

Heading through a dense forest of old-growth Sitka spruce with an understory of ferns, salal, and salmonberry, openings in the trees offer views to the south of a secluded beach accessible via the South Trail junction at the beginning of the hike.

At about .6 miles in, a marker commemorates a World War II B-17 bomber that crashed nearby. At 1.2 miles in, a railed overlook provides views to the north, showing the waves crashing below at the edge of the cape. A couple of sections of the trail are along open cliffs with 400 feet drop-offs, so be careful to watch your step here. Several additional sections offer views to the north of Cape Meares, Three Arch Rocks, Netarts Spit, and the campground at Cape Lookout State Park.

The end of the cape is railed, with views to the north obstructed by trees, but the views of the ocean stretch out endlessly westward, and to the south look out toward Cape Kiwanda and Cascade Head.

Gray whales migrate close to shore from December to June, and this is one of the best locations in Oregon to view them as they detour around the cape. Return the same way.

Distance: 5.2 miles (roundtrip)

Elevation Gain: 450 ft.

Difficulty: easy to moderate

Hike type: out and back

Trail: packed dirt and boardwalks, often muddy

Typically open: all year

Best time of year: all year, except during winter storms

Features: ocean views, coastal forest, whale watching

Fees/permits: Oregon State Parks day use fee

Agency: Cape Lookout State Park, Oregon State Parks (see pg. 126)

ON AUGUST 1,1943 A FOUR MOTORED
ARMY AIR FORCE PLANE CRASHED 500
WEST OF HERE. THIS MARKER ERECTED
THE OREGON STATE HIGHWAY COMMISS
IN COMMEMORATION OF THE MEMBERS O
THIS FLIGHT CREW THAT PERISHED IN
THE LINE OF DUTY.

PILOT	ROY JAMES LEE	2ND
CO-PILOT	ROBERT W. WILKINS	2ND
NAVIGATOR	VICTOR A. LOWENFELDT	2ND
BOMBARDIER (SURVIVOR)	WILBUR L. PEREZ	2ND
AERIAL ENG. G.	DELMAR R. PRIEST	S/
ASST. AERIAL ENG. G.	WILLIAM M. PRUNER	SGT
RADIO OPER. G.	BENJAMIN J. POZIO	SGT
ASST RADIO OPER. G.	PAUL W. MANDEVILLE	SGT
ARMORER GUNNER	HARRY LILLEY	S/
ASST. ARM. G.	HOYT W. WILSON	S/

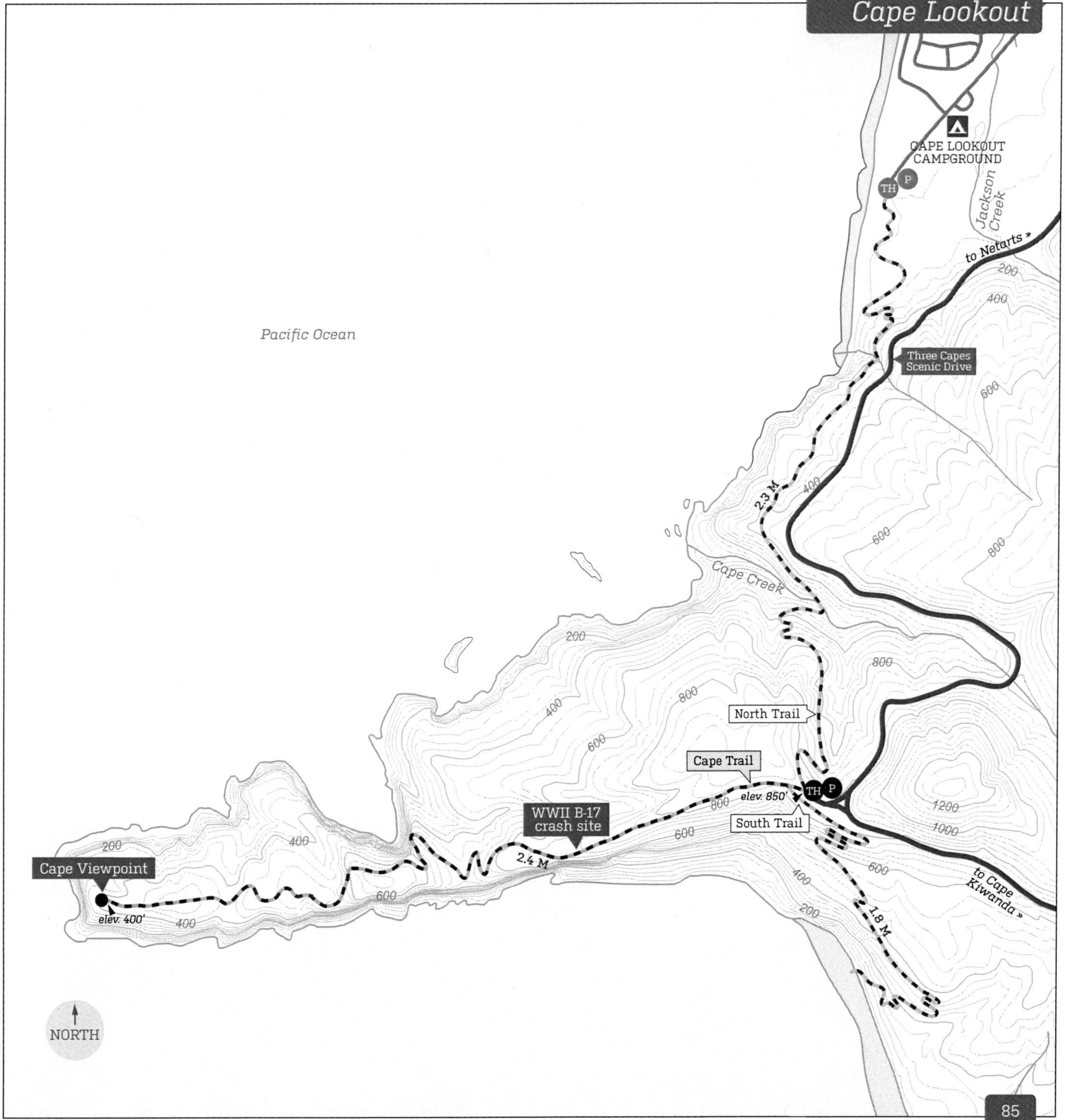

Pacific Ocean

to Netarts »

CAPE LOOKOUT
CAMPGROUND

TH P

Jackson Creek

200

400

Three Capes
Scenic Drive

600

800

2.3 M

400

Cape Creek

200

600

800

400

North Trail

800

Cape Trail

elev. 850'   TH P

1200

1000

WWII B-17
crash site

South Trail

600

2.4 M

800

600

400

to Cape
Kiwanda »

200

600

Cape Viewpoint

elev. 400'   400

200

400

600

1.8 M

NORTH

Located on the Oregon Coast's Three Capes Scenic Loop, Netarts Spit is accessed via Cape Lookout State Park. The spit is a 5-mile long narrow section of beach that separates Netarts Bay from the ocean.

DIRECTIONS

From Portland, drive west for 20 miles on Highway 26 to the Highway 6 exit.

Stay to the left and continue on Highway 6 for 50 miles through the Coast Range to Tillamook.

At the Hwy 101 junction in Tillamook, follow signs for Cape Lookout State Park, continuing straight on 1st St.

Turn left on Birch St., then right on 3rd St., which becomes Netarts Highway.

Continue on Netarts Highway for 4.5 miles.

Following signs for Cape Lookout State Park, turn left at Whiskey Creek Road.

Continue for about 6 miles to the Cape Lookout State Park entrance, and follow signs to the day use area.

Drive time from Portland: 1 hour 45 minutes

THE HIKE

Spits are long, narrow landforms developed by the movement and accumulation of beach material due to waves traveling at an angle to the coast. They occur where the coastline changes direction, forming a shallow protected area of water. In this case, Netarts Bay and its narrow mud flats are what formed Netarts Spit.

Cape Lookout State Park includes a large campground with yurts, cabins and sites for tents and RVs. The day use area provides access to the park's seven miles of beach and many trails for hiking. To prevent erosion, European beach grass was planted here and along other low areas on the Oregon coast, which created small foredunes. Paths cut through the dunes at the park for beach access. Since part of the beach gets cut off during high tides, plan to do this hike at low tide.

Even though there's no elevation gain on this hike, it's still a good workout because walking on sand exerts more muscle effort than walking on a hard surface.

Begin the hike at the day use area, following an access trail to the beach, and head north for five miles to the end of the spit. The two-mile-long basalt headland of Cape Lookout is at the south end of the beach, and Netarts Spit heads north, all the way to the opening of Netarts Bay. Along the beach, the bay is hidden from site by short dunes, but there are several areas along the dune to climb up for a view of the bay and Coastal Mountains behind it.

To the north, the small beach communities of Oceanside and Netarts are visible. About a half-mile off the coastline, Three Arch Rocks National Wildlife Refuge provides protection for more than 150 species of birds, including Oregon's largest breeding colony of tufted puffins, and is a pupping site for the threatened Stellar sea lion.

At the end of the spit where the ocean and the bay meet, the waves change direction, angling towards shore, splashing into small pools of water along the shoreline. At the tip of the cape, harbor seals sometimes gather to sun, and at low tides, the bay's mud flats are a popular spot for clamming.

Distance: 10.6 miles (roundtrip)

Elevation Gain: none

Difficulty: easy to moderate

Hike type: out and back

Trail: beach

Typical open: all year

Best time of year: all year, except during winter storms

Features: beach, ocean views, bay

Fees/permits: Oregon State Parks day use fee

Agency: Cape Lookout State Park, Oregon State Parks (see pg. 126)

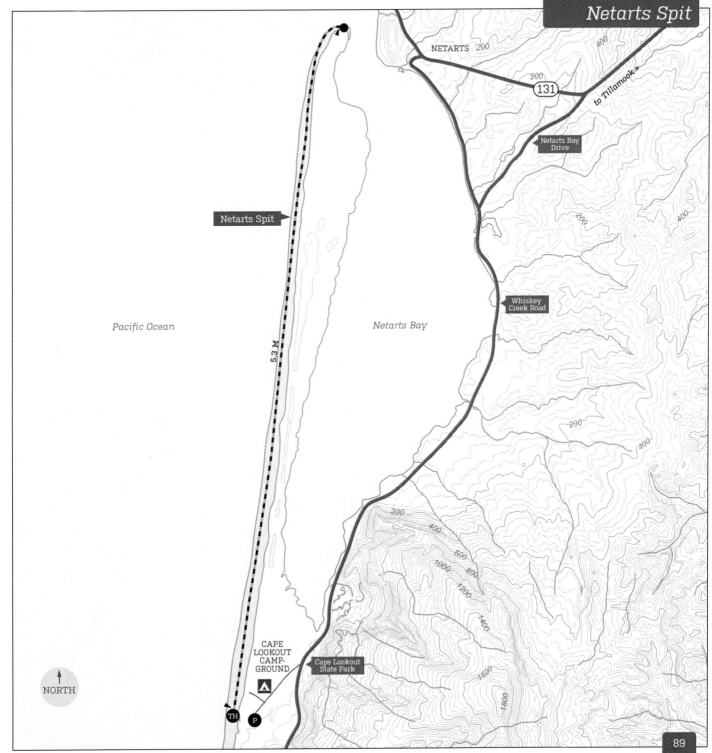

NETARTS 200

131

to Tillamook →

Netarts Bay Drive

Whiskey Creek Road

Netarts Spit

Pacific Ocean

5.3 M

Netarts Bay

CAPE LOOKOUT CAMP- GROUND

Cape Lookout State Park

TH

P

NORTH

Take one of three hikes at Ecola State Park – one of the most scenic sections along the Oregon Coast – to secluded Crescent beach, to Indian Beach, or follow a route on Tillamook Head taken by Lewis and Clark.

DIRECTIONS

From Portland, drive 74 miles west on Highway 26.

Take the US 101 South exit (Oregon Coast Highway).

Continue for 3 miles to the first exit for Cannon Beach.

Turn right, and just past the stop sign, turn right at a sign for Ecola State Park.

Follow this road for 1.5 miles to the entry booth for day use payment.

Turn left to park at Ecola Point, or continue for another 1.5 miles to the parking area at Indian Beach.

Drive time from Portland: 1 hour 30 minutes

THE HIKES

Ecola State Park is located on the north end of Cannon Beach, a charming beach town filled with shops, restaurants, and art galleries. The name Ecola originates from the Chinook tribe's word for whale: "ekoli." Lewis and Clark crossed the headland at Tillamook Head in 1806 to purchase whale blubber from the local tribes at what is now Cannon Beach.

The park was originally developed by the Civilian Conservation Corps and includes two parking areas for beach and hiking trail access. Park at Ecola Point to access the Crescent Beach hike, which is only accessible via the 1.2 mile descent to the secluded beach.

Crescent Beach hike: park at Ecola Point and look for the trailhead near the restrooms. This secluded beach is one of the most photographed places in Oregon. Bounded on the north by Ecola Point and on the south by Chapman Point, this pocket beach is only accessible via the 1.2 mile hike down a steep and often muddy trail, making it more isolated than most beaches on the northern coast.

Ecola Point to Indian Beach hike: park at either Ecola Point or Indian Beach for this 1.5 mile hike along the coastline through old-growth coastal rainforest. The trail is often muddy and after winter storms has a lot of blowdown, so trail conditions sometimes require climbing up and around obstructions. Regardless, the views along this hike are well worth the effort.

Tillamook Head hike: this massive basalt headland and the trail continue all the way to Seaside, Oregon, and were part of the route taken by Lewis and Clark. Like Cape Lookout (hike 16), Tillamook Head was formed by the massive lava flows 15 million years ago as they spread out over the coastline. About 1.5 miles in is a hikers' camp with three open-sided shelters. A fork in the trail leads to a viewpoint looking out towards Tillamook Lighthouse, more than a mile off the coastline, and passes a World War II bunker built to protect the west coast. For a loop, take the wider "Clatsop Loop" road back to Indian Beach.

CRESCENT BEACH
Distance: 2.4 miles (roundtrip)
Elevation Gain: 200 ft.
Difficulty: easy to moderate

ECOLA POINT TO INDIAN BEACH
Distance: 3 miles (roundtrip)
Elevation Gain: 200 ft.
Difficulty: easy

TILLAMOOK HEAD
Distance: 3.2 miles (roundtrip)
Elevation Gain: 800 ft.
Difficulty: moderate

Hike types: out and back

Trails: packed dirt (often muddy)

Best time of year: all year, except during winter storms

Features: coastal forest, ocean views, beaches, whale watching

Fees/permits: Oregon State Parks day use fee

Agency: Ecola State Park, Oregon State Parks (see pg. 126)

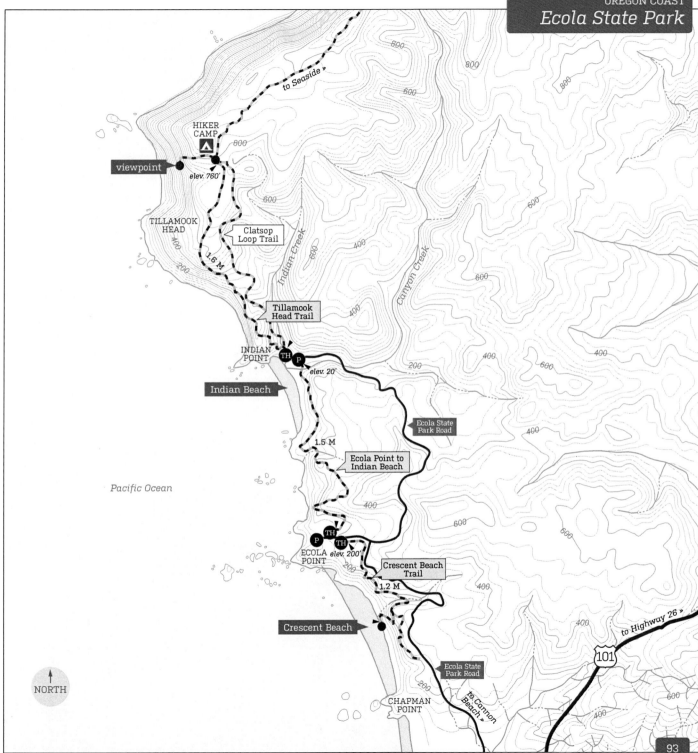

to Seaside »

800

800

600

HIKER
CAMP

800

600

viewpoint

elev. 760'

TILLAMOOK
HEAD

600

600

Clatsop
Loop Trail

400

Indian Creek

Canyon Creek

200

1.6 M

400

Tillamook
Head Trail

INDIAN
POINT

TH P

elev. 20'

200

400

400

Indian Beach

400

600

1.5 M

Ecola State
Park Road

Ecola Point to
Indian Beach

Pacific Ocean

400

600

600

TH

ECOLA
POINT

P

TH

elev. 200'

200

Crescent Beach
Trail

400

1.2 M

to Highway 26 »

Crescent Beach

200

101

400

600

NORTH

Ecola State
Park Road

to Cannon
Beach »

CHAPMAN
POINT

200

400

600

Southwest Washington

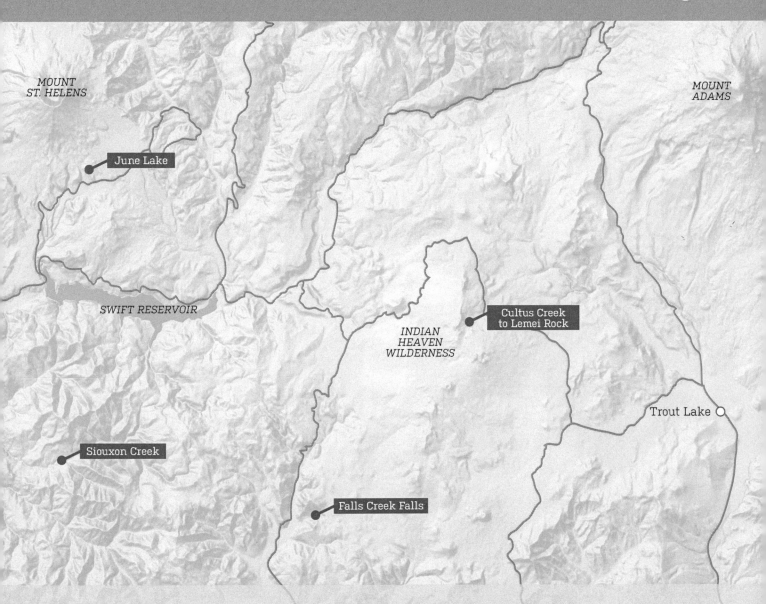

MOUNT
ST. HELENS

MOUNT
ADAMS

June Lake

SWIFT RESERVOIR

INDIAN
HEAVEN
WILDERNESS

Cultus Creek
to Lemei Rock

Trout Lake

Siouxon Creek

Falls Creek Falls

Southwest Washington is often overlooked by hikers in the Portland area, but there are many outstanding places to explore between the Columbia River and the high mountains of Washington's southern Cascades. Located within the Gifford Pinchot National Forest, the hikes in this area offer everything from lush green lower elevation forests with waterfalls and creeks to high plateau alpine meadows and lakes with views of nearby Mount St. Helens, Mount Rainier, and Mount Adams.

Stunning Falls Creek Falls is the highlight of this loop hike that combines an easy hike alongside a mossy creek in old-growth forest with an upper ridge trail and canyon views.

DIRECTIONS

From Portland, drive east on I-84 to exit 44 for Cascade Locks.

Turn right at the sign for Bridge of the Gods. Go across the bridge, paying $1 toll.

Turn right onto Highway 14 and continue for 5.9 miles.

Turn left on Wind River Road 30. Go through the small town of Carson, continuing for 14.5 miles.

At a sign for Wind River Road 30, turn right and continue for .8 miles to Road 3062.

Turn right, continuing on Road 3062 for 2 miles.

Fork right at Road 057 at a sign for Lower Falls Creek Falls to a large parking area.

Drive time from Portland: 1 hour 30 minutes

THE HIKE

Following Falls Creek, after the first half-mile cross a cable suspension bridge which spans the creek at a narrow gorge. From here, the trail enters an old-growth forest of western red cedar and Douglas fir. In autumn the understory of vine maple turns brilliant shades of yellow, orange, and red.

Alongside the trail, there are several areas where you can scramble down to explore the creek up close. Continuing along the trail, it begins to climb higher above the creek. Continue past a connector trail to the Upper Falls Creek trail. To do the loop, you'll track back to this junction. For now, head straight on the trail.

Soon after, you will begin to hear the roar of Falls Creek Falls (200 ft.). The upper tier of the three-tier waterfall is visible through the trees. At the base of the falls, only the bottom two tiers are visible. Large boulders in an open wooded area provide plenty of seating to soak in the views.

To continue the full loop, go back about 0.3 miles to the junction with the upper trail and head up the steep trail for 0.2 miles, then turn right on the Upper Falls Creek trail. The upper trail is open to equestrians and continues east for about four more miles to the Falls Creek Horse Camp at Forest Road 65.

After hiking a little over half a mile along this forested ridge-trail high above the creek, begin looking for faint side trails to the right. Several of these lead to cliff-edge views of the Falls Creek canyon and limited views of the waterfall.

If you wish, continue along the trail a short distance to another canyon viewpoint near the top of the waterfall, then turn around and return the same way, passing the junction trail and continuing on the gently declining trail for just over 1.5 miles to a side trail leading to a bridge over Falls Creek. Turn left here and go another 0.6 miles to return to the parking lot.

Distance: 6.3 miles (roundtrip)

Elevation Gain: 1,150 ft.

Difficulty: moderate

Hike type: loop

Trail: packed dirt

Typically open: April 1 to Nov. 30

Best time of year: May - June

Features: waterfall, creeks, canyon view

Fees/permits: none

Agency: Mount Adams Ranger District, Gifford Pinchot National Forest (see pg. 126)

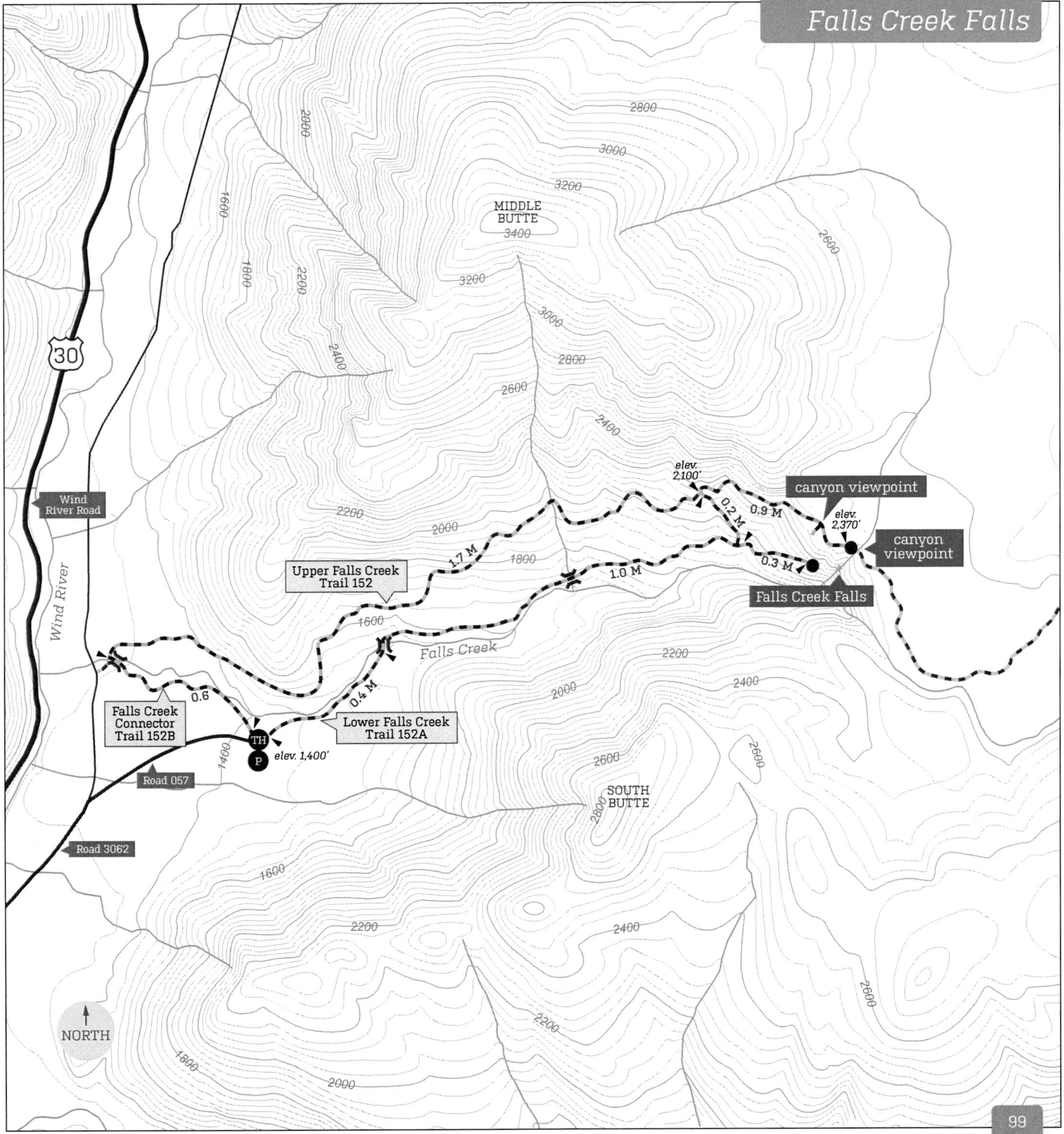

2800
3000
3200
3400
2600

MIDDLE
BUTTE
3400

3200

3000

2800

2600

2400

2200

2000

1800

1600

30

Wind River Road

Wind River

*elev.
2,100'*

canyon viewpoint

0.2 M

0.9 M

*elev.
2,370'*

canyon
viewpoint

1.7 M

Upper Falls Creek
Trail 152

1.0 M

0.3 M

Falls Creek Falls

Falls Creek

0.6

0.4 M

Falls Creek
Connector
Trail 152B

Lower Falls Creek
Trail 152A

TH
P
elev. 1,400'

Road 057

SOUTH
BUTTE

Road 3062

NORTH

Indian Heaven Wilderness is a high plateau full of alpine lakes and meadows filled with huckleberry and heather, which turn brilliant shades of red and orange in late autumn.

DIRECTIONS

From Portland, drive east on Highway 84 to exit 44 for Cascade Locks.

Turn right at the sign for Bridge of the Gods. Go across the bridge, paying $1 toll.

Turn right onto Highway 14 and continue for 5.9 miles.

Turn left on Wind River Road 30. Go through the small town of Carson, continuing for 14.5 miles.

At a sign for Wind River Road 30, turn right and continue for 15.8 miles.

The pavement ends near a sign for Lone Butte Sno-Park. Stay to the right, continuing on Lone Butte Road 30 for 7.9 miles

Turn right at gravel Road 24 for 4.1 miles to Cultus Creek campground. Park at the south end of the campground by a sign for Indian Heaven Trail 33.

Drive time from Portland: 2 hours 30 minutes

THE HIKE

Indian Heaven Wilderness is a truly special place. Native American tribes gathered here annually for almost 10,000 years to gather the plentiful huckleberries, fish in the 150+ small lakes that dot the region, hunt, trade, race horses, and celebrate together. Through a rare handshake agreement in 1932 by the Yakima Nation and the Forest Service, the Sawtooth Berry Fields on the north end of the wilderness were designated exclusively to be used by local tribes.

The area is generally snow free by mid-July, but the swarms of mosquitos in the summer make this area known as "mosquito heaven." Fall is a much better season to hike here due to the abundance of huckleberries and heather that literally cover the entire area with stunning colors.

This hike begins at the south end of the Cultus Creek campground near a sign for "Indian Heaven Trail No. 33 Parking Area." The first 1.5 miles of trail steeply climb up the side of Bird Mountain through thick Douglas fir forest. At about one mile in, an opening in the ridge offers outstanding views of Mount Adams to the east, with Mount Rainier, Goat Rocks, and Sawtooth Mountain visible to the north. The trail levels out near the base of Bird Mountain and goes through several sections of pine forest and open meadow before reaching the splendid alpine beauty of Cultus Lake. A short side trail just before this leads to Deep Lake.

At the trail junction past Cultus Lake, turn left on the Lake Wapiki Trail and continue just over a mile through several open meadows with stands of noble and Pacific silver fir to Lemei Rock, an ancient volcanic crag and the highest point in the Wilderness. Go past Lemei Rock and through an uphill wooded area to an opening with a view down towards Lake Wapiki, a bright blue lake that sits in an old cinder cone. Views of Mount Adams dominate to the east. You can continue another mile to the lake, or turn around and return the same way.

Distance: 6.8 miles (roundtrip)

Elevation Gain: 1,500 ft.

Difficulty: moderate to difficult

Hike type: out and back

Trail: packed dirt

Typically open: mid-July - mid-Oct.

Best time of year: Sept. - Oct.

Features: fall color, alpine meadows, lakes, mountain views

Fees/permits: Northwest Forest Pass required

Agency: Mount Adams Ranger District, Gifford Pinchot National Forest (see pg. 126)

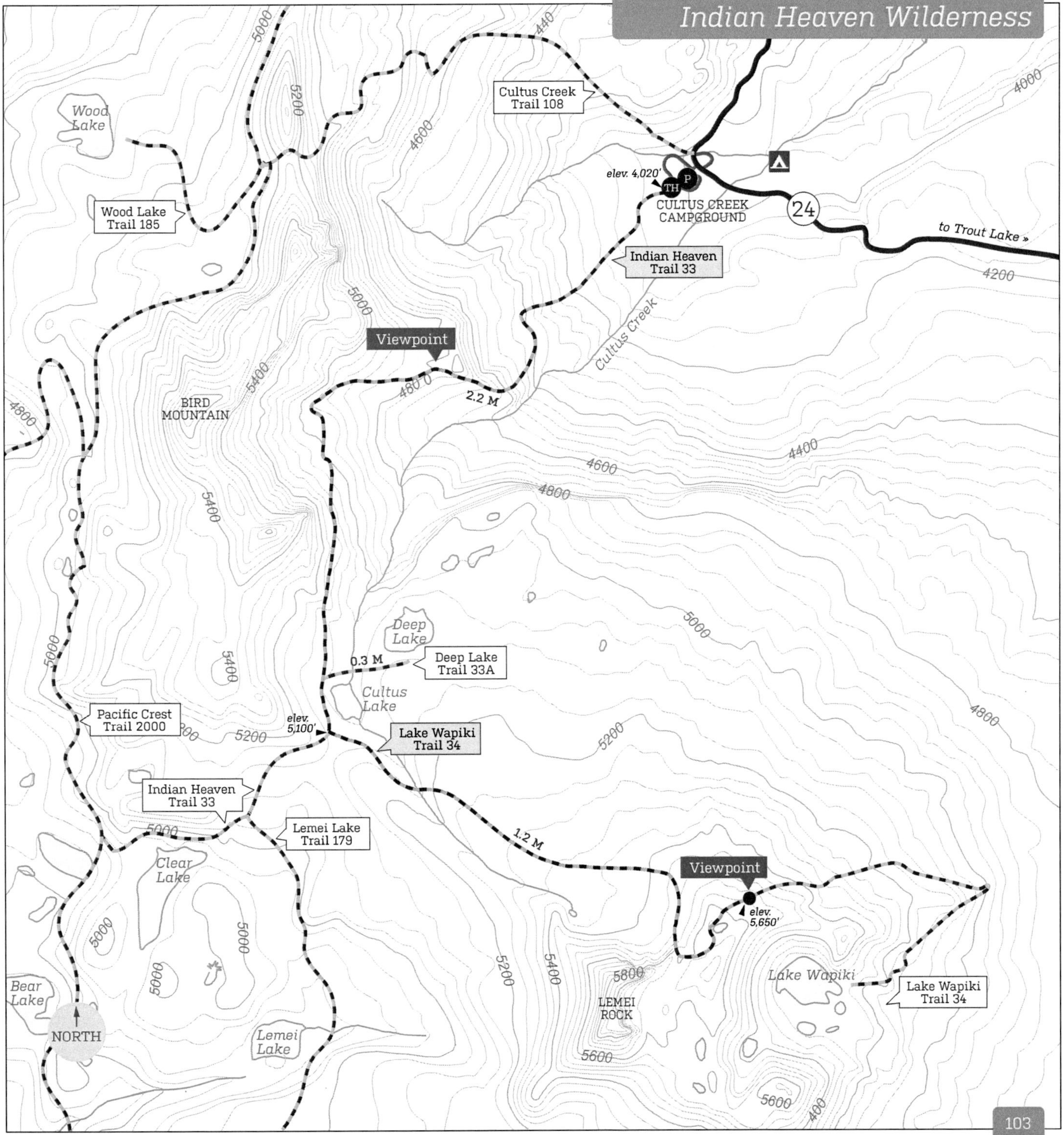

Wood Lake

Cultus Creek
Trail 108

5200

4600

440

4000

Wood Lake
Trail 185

elev. 4,020'

TH P

CULTUS CREEK
CAMPGROUND

4200

to Trout Lake »

24

Indian Heaven
Trail 33

5000

Cultus Creek

4200

Viewpoint

4800

2.2 M

BIRD
MOUNTAIN

5400

4800

4600

4800

4400

5200

5000

Deep
Lake

0.3 M

Deep Lake
Trail 33A

5400

Cultus
Lake

Pacific Crest
Trail 2000

5200

elev. 5,100'

Lake Wapiki
Trail 34

4800

5200

Indian Heaven
Trail 33

5000

1.2 M

Lemei Lake
Trail 179

Clear
Lake

Viewpoint

elev. 5,650'

5000

5000

5200

5400

5800

Lake Wapiki

Lake Wapiki
Trail 34

Bear
Lake

6000

NORTH

Lemei
Lake

5200

LEMEI
ROCK

5600

5600

400

The trail beside Siouxon Creek and its stunning waterfalls travels through an amazing forest lush with many shades of green: ferns, mosses and lichens, emerald pools of water, and towering conifers.

DIRECTIONS

From Portland, drive east on I-84 for 5.7 miles to Exit 8 for I-205 North.

Continue on I-205 for 7.8 miles, crossing the Columbia River and entering Washington.

Take the Highway 500 Exit 30A, 30B and 30C, then stay to the left for 30B Highway 500 E.

Continue for 26.2 miles, driving through Battle Ground where Highway 500 becomes Highway 503.

Just after the town of Amboy, turn right to stay on Highway 503.

Just past the Mount St. Helens National Monument Headquarters, turn right on NE Healy Road.

Set your odometer at each of the following segments since the roads are unmarked.

Continue on NE Healy Road, which becomes Forest Road 54, for 9.2 miles to a fork, turning left on FR 57.

Continue on FR 57 for 1.2 miles, turning left on FR 5701..

Continue on FR 5701 for 4.8 miles to the parking area for the Siouxon Creek Trail just before the road ends.

Drive time from Portland: 1 hour 40 minutes

THE HIKE

Located south of Mount St. Helens in the Gifford Pinchot National Forest, the trail starts by going downhill for about 50 feet, then heads towards Siouxon (pronounced "SOO-sahn") Creek. Before reaching the creek (which is as large as many rivers in the region), cross a small tributary creek on a one-rail flat log bridge. A short distance ahead, an open section of rustic campsites sits between the trail and creek, making for a great backpacking destination.

The forest floor is covered with "nurse" logs, fallen trees that decay and provide nourishment to the forest, many times with new trees rooting over them.

At about 1.5 miles in, Horsetail Creek Falls (57 ft.) is a lovely fan-shaped waterfall that spills down black basalt rock in three tiers. A small bridge crosses the creek above the waterfall over a narrow rocky gorge with an emerald green pool of water. A short distance ahead is Siouxon Falls (28 ft.), a thundering cataract waterfall with a wide bowl-shaped deep pool. Just past the waterfall is a side trail that leads to an open area next to the creek, good for exploring a rocky section in the water at the top of the waterfall.

Continue on the main trail, skirting above the creek and through boggy lower sections of forest, passing a lower wide waterfall across the creek. Numerous side trails lead to more campsites, or good places to spend a little time enjoying the scenery. At 3.7 miles is a view of another deep emerald green pool just before a trail junction and a bridge over a split in the creek. Before the bridge is a small tributary with a wide section of rock that can be slippery and difficult to cross in high water. Once past this rocky water crossing, turn left on the trail to cross the bridge. Continue on the trail until it ends near the creek to view dramatic Chinook Falls (62 ft.).

Continuing on the trail requires fording the creek to the trail on the other side, so this is a good place to end the hike before returning the same way.

Distance: 7.7 miles (roundtrip)

Elevation Gain: 700 ft.

Difficulty: easy to moderate

Hike type: out and back

Trail: packed dirt

Typically open: March - Nov.

Best time of year: April - May

Features: waterfalls, creeks, forest

Fees/permits: none

Agency: Gifford Pinchot National Forest (see pg. 126)

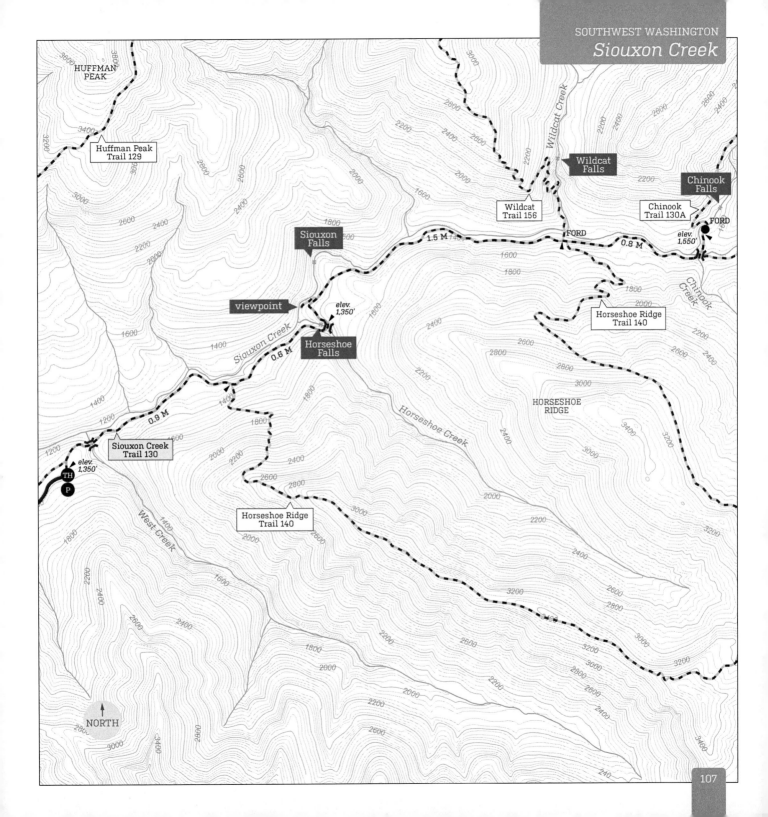

HUFFMAN PEAK

Huffman Peak
Trail 129

Wildcat Creek

Wildcat
Falls

Chinook
Falls

Wildcat
Trail 156

Chinook
Trail 130A

FORD

elev.
1,550'

Siouxon
Falls

1.5 M

FORD

0.8 M

Chinook Creek

viewpoint

elev.
1,350'

Horseshoe Ridge
Trail 140

Siouxon Creek

0.6 M

Horseshoe
Falls

Horseshoe Creek

HORSESHOE
RIDGE

0.9 M

Siouxon Creek
Trail 130

elev.
1,350'

TH

P

West Creek

Horseshoe Ridge
Trail 140

NORTH

Hike to a shallow lake with a waterfall near the timberline on the south side of Mount St. Helens and continue on to explore ancient lava fields at the base of the mountain.

DIRECTIONS

From Portland, drive north on I-5 for 25 miles to exit 21 for WA 503 Woodland/Cougar.

Turn right and drive east for 35 miles (6.7 miles past the town of Cougar).

Turn left at NF-83, following signs for Ape Cave and Lava Canyon.

Drive 7.2 miles on NF-83 and turn left at a sign for the June Lake trailhead.

Drive time from Portland: 1 hour 45 minutes

THE HIKE

The May 18, 1980 eruption of Mount St. Helens forever changed the landscape around the mountain. However, most of the blast impacted the north side of the mountain, leaving the south side relatively untouched. And it's on the mountain's south side, not far from June Lake, where hikers planning to summit the rim begin their trip.

This hike begins at the June Lake Trailhead and parallels June Creek, with several side trails worth exploring near the trailhead that lead to the creek bed and views of the south side of Mount St. Helens. The trail climbs gradually through the forest, with occasional openings and views along the way.

After crossing the creek on a small bridge, enter a wide, sandy plain with small shrubbery, the site of an ancient mudflow. Lava flows on the south side of the mountain are visible to the north. To the east lies the June Lake basin, surrounded by old-growth western hemlock covering the cliff ridge around the lake.

A 40 ft. waterfall along the edge of this shallow lake begins as a spring just above the edge of a lava field. After leaving June Lake, the trail switchbacks up to connect with the Loowit Trail. From here, you can head in either direction through lava fields. The 30-mile Loowit Trail circumnavigates all the way around Mount St. Helens. Turn right at the junction to hike through the lava formations known as the worm flows, formed by ancient lava flows that rolled and solidified, with more lava flowing over it and solidifying again and again.

Return the same way.

Optional hike: Turn left at the Loowit Trail junction and hike for about 1.3 miles through large boulder-filled lava fields to Chocolate Falls, named for the color of the ash-filled water that resembles chocolate milk.

Distance: 4 miles (roundtrip)

Elevation Gain: 750 ft

Difficulty: easy to moderate

Hike type: out and back

Trail: packed dirt, ash and lava rock

Typically open: June - Nov.

Best time of year: July - Oct.

Features: mountain views, lake, waterfall, geologic features

Fees/permits: Northwest Forest Pass required

Agency: Mount St. Helens National Monument (see pg. 126)

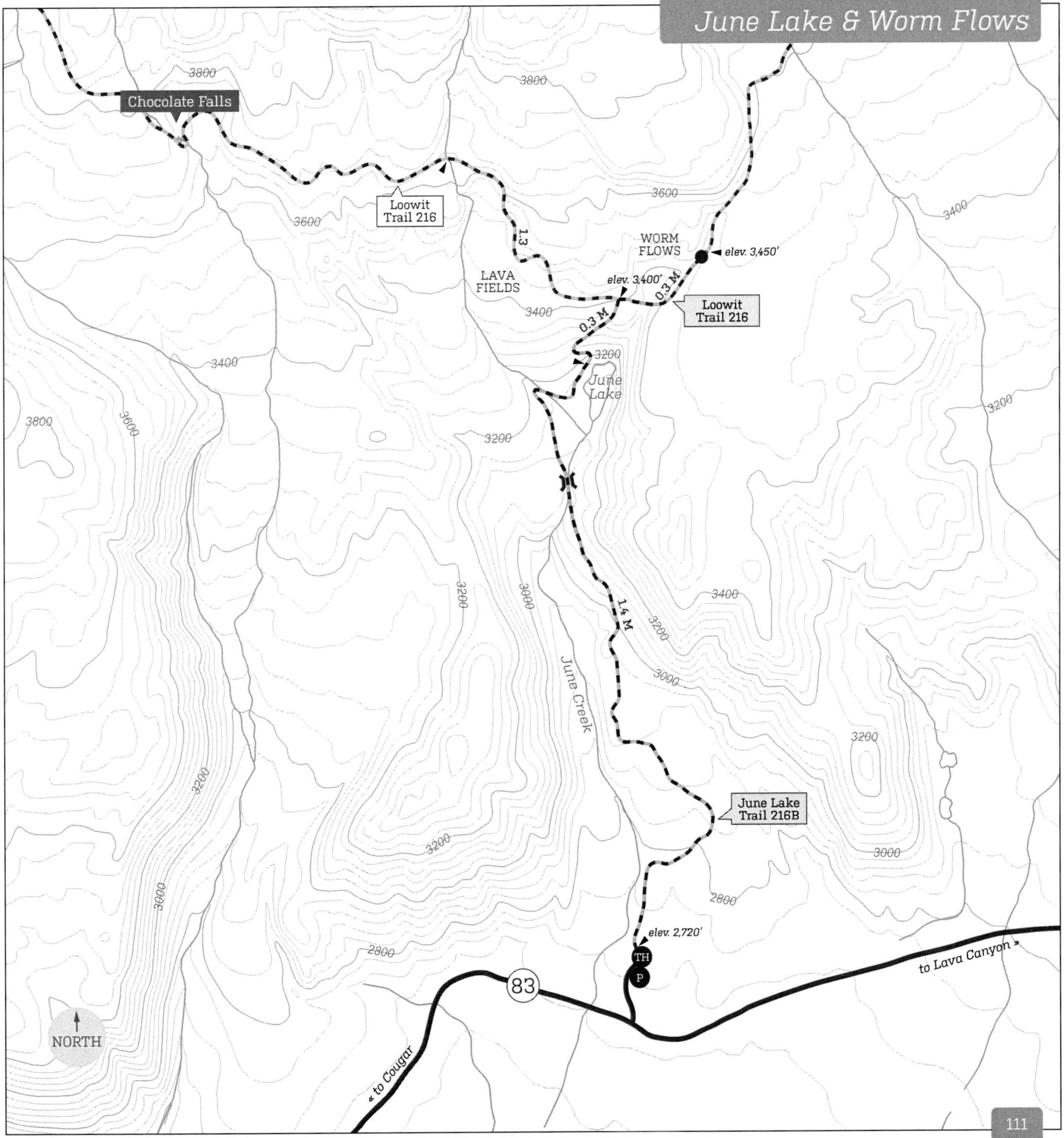

Chocolate Falls
3800
3800
Loowit Trail 216
3600
3600
1.3
WORM FLOWS
elev. 3,450'
LAVA FIELDS
elev. 3,400'
0.3 M
0.3 M
Loowit Trail 216
3400
3400
3400
3200
June Lake
3800
3600
3200
3200
3200
3000
1.4 M
3400
3200
June Creek
3000
3200
3200
June Lake Trail 216B
3200
3000
3000
2800
elev. 2,720'
2800
TH
P
83
to Lava Canyon »
NORTH
« to Cougar

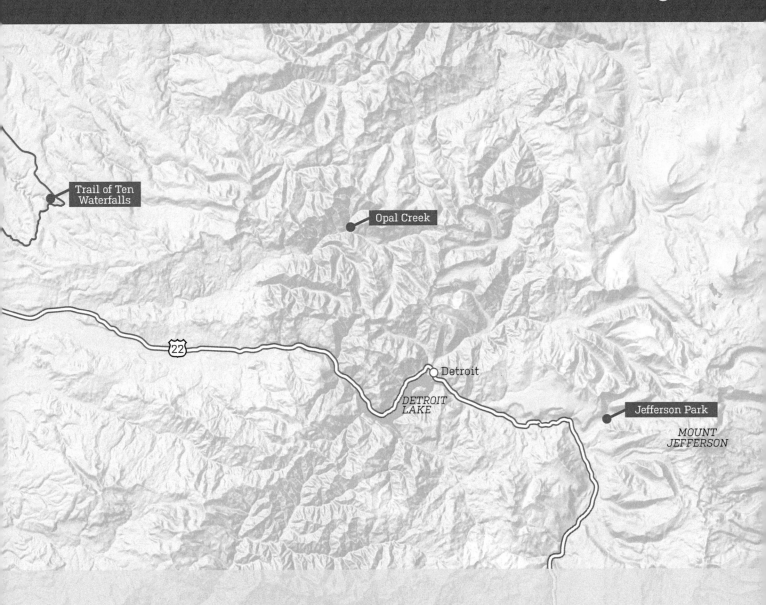

Trail of Ten
Waterfalls

Opal Creek

22

Detroit

DETROIT
LAKE

Jefferson Park

MOUNT
JEFFERSON

Although located farther from Portland than other regions in this book, the hikes in the Willamette-Santiam region are accessible due to their location next to the I-5 corridor, with highways running east to Central Oregon. The area includes the lush waterfall-filled canyon of Silver Falls State Park, the previously threatened old-growth forest of Opal Creek, and Oregon's second highest Cascade peak, Mount Jefferson.

The Trail of Ten Waterfalls hike in Silver Falls State Park is a waterfall lover's dream. It's popular and crowded, but with more waterfalls that can be seen on any hike in the region and beautiful creeks running through the entire canyon, it is well worth a visit.

DIRECTIONS

From Portland, drive south on I-5 for 17 miles to Woodburn exit 271.

Turn left (east) on Highway 214 and drive 2 miles to the junction with Highway 99E.

Turn right (south), then 1.5 miles to a junction with a continuation of Highway 214 at a stoplight.

Turn left (east) and drive 28 miles, going through the town of Silverton, following signs for Silver Falls State Park.

After entering the park, drive 2.3 miles to the main extra large parking area.

Drive time from Portland: 1 hour 40 minutes

THE HIKE

The largest state park in Oregon, Silver Falls includes a large campground, a lodge built in the 1930s by the Civilian Conservation Corps, picnic areas, a conference center, and trails for hiking, horseback riding and bicycling.

Begin this hike at the main trailhead at the busy south end of the park. South Falls (177 ft.), like several of the waterfalls here, has a cavern with a path going behind the waterfall. Walking behind a powerful wall of water is always impressive! The caverns were created by basalt lava that flowed over softer, older rock then hardened. Over time, the softer layers eroded, leaving pathways in these carved out spaces. The paths here are paved, but once you get past South Falls, the trail changes to a packed dirt and gravel path and the crowds thin out.

Continue for just over a half-mile, then descend several switchbacks of stairs to access Lower South Falls (93 ft.), another walk-behind waterfall. A junction with the Maple Ridge Trail allows for a shorter 2.8 mile loop option. For the short option, turn here and head back to the South Falls. Otherwise, continue on the main trail for about another mile to Lower North Falls (30 ft.). A short side trail leads to Double Falls (178 ft.). Back on the main trail, a wooden platform provides a view of Drake Falls (27 ft.), named for Silverton photographer June Drake, who worked for 20 years to get the area designated as a park. Next comes Middle North Falls (106 ft.), which also has a walk-behind cavern accessible via a short side trail.

If opting for a shorter 5.2 mile loop, turn right at the bridge after Middle North Falls and cut through the canyon to Winter Falls. For the full longer loop, continue straight on the trail to Twin Falls (31 ft.), then to spectacular North Falls (136 ft.). Take the short trail crossing under the highway to view secluded Upper North Falls (65 ft.) before heading back along the Rim Trail to Winter Falls (134 ft.). From here, follow the trail through a lovely wooded area with an understory of ferns, Oregon grape and salal back to the parking lot.

Distance: 7.7 miles (roundtrip)

Elevation Gain: 700 ft.

Difficulty: easy to moderate

Hike type: loop

Trail: packed dirt

Typically open: all year

Best time of year: all year

Features: waterfalls, creeks

Fees/permits: Oregon State Park day use fee

Agency: Silver Falls State Park, Oregon State Parks (see pg. 126)

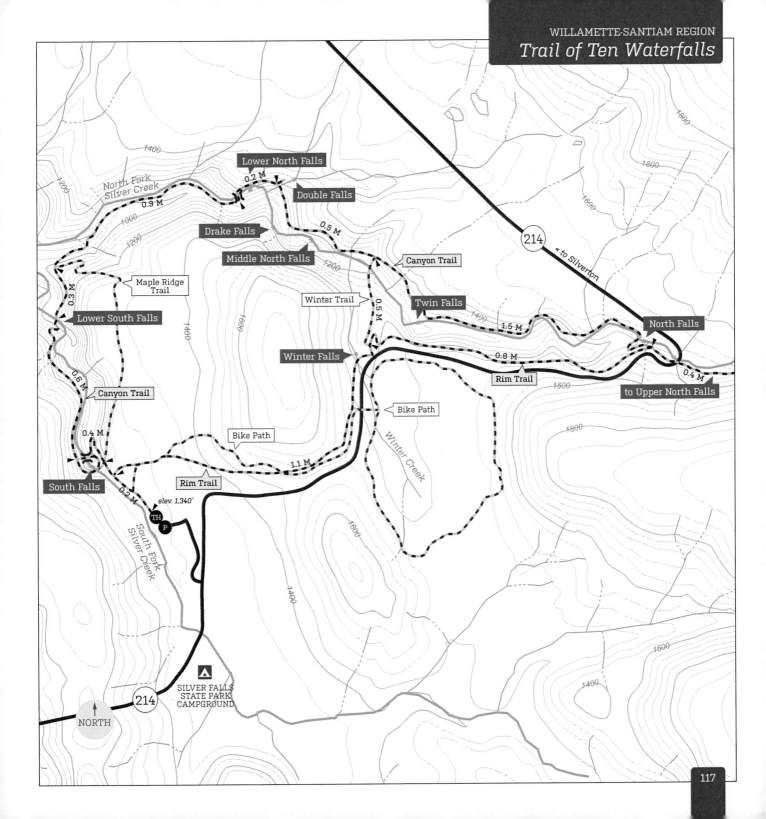

Lower North Falls

0.2 M

Double Falls

North Fork Silver Creek

0.9 M

0.5 M

Drake Falls

Middle North Falls

Canyon Trail

Maple Ridge Trail

0.3 M

Winter Trail

Twin Falls

214

← to Silverton

Lower South Falls

0.5 M

North Falls

0.6 M

Winter Falls

1.5 M

Canyon Trail

0.8 M

Rim Trail

to Upper North Falls

0.4 M

0.4 M

Bike Path

Bike Path

Winter Creek

South Falls

1.1 M

0.2 M

Rim Trail

elev. 1,340'

TH
P

South Fork Silver Creek

SILVER FALLS
STATE PARK
CAMPGROUND

214

NORTH

Jefferson Park is a remarkable alpine meadow and lake-filled basin at the base of Mount Jefferson. The Whitewater Trail provides one of the shortest and easiest routes to this premier area.

DIRECTIONS

From Portland, drive south on I-5 for 46 miles to the Highway 22 Detroit Lake/ Bend exit.

Turn left and drive east on Highway 22 (North Santiam Highway) for 59.2 miles, passing through Detroit, to Forest Road 2243.

Turn left on Forest Road 2243 (Whitewater Road) and continue for 7.6 miles to the trailhead and parking area.

Drive time from Portland: 2 hours 20 minutes

THE HIKE

At 10,497 ft., Mount Jefferson is the second highest peak in Oregon. Unlike Mount Hood to the north, Mount Jefferson is located in a roadless wilderness area, accessible only via hiking trails on the north, west, and south sides of the mountain. The eastern portion of the mountain is within the Warm Springs Indian Reservation.

The alpine meadows of Jefferson Park are about one mile wide and three miles long at 5,800 ft. elevation, just below the glaciers on the northern side of Mount Jefferson. Conifer forests of Douglas fir, silver fir, mountain hemlock, lodgepole pine, ponderosa pine, and several types of cedar mix with an understory of vine maples, rhododendrons, and beargrass. Wildflowers include Indian paintbrush, wild strawberries, blue lupines, and heathers.

The area is usually snow-free from mid-July to October, but mosquitos can be heavy after snow melt until early August. Autumn is a great time to visit, with huckleberry shrubs in vivid shades of red and orange. Popular with backpackers, camping is permitted only in designated areas due to heavy usage, and campfires are banned.

Begin the hike at the Whitewater trailhead, climbing moderately through forest for the first 1.5 miles. At a trail junction, turn right on a ridge and continue for another 2.7 miles, with occasional openings in the forest that provide incredible views of Mount Jefferson. Cross Whitewater Creek just before a junction with the Pacific Crest Trail. Stay to the left here, heading towards Jefferson Park. For the next mile, the trail gets even more scenic, with small wildflower-filled meadows and several stream crossings, before leveling out near the alpine basin.

Multiple side trails in this area offer exploration of the many alpine lakes that dot Jefferson Park. A well worn but unmarked side trail leads to Scout Lake and continues to the steep rocky shoreline of Bays Lake. After enjoying all that this area has to offer, return the same way.

Conditions in higher elevations can change rapidly, so be prepared for rain, high winds, snow, or ice in any season.

Distance: 10.4 miles (roundtrip)

Elevation Gain: 1,800 ft.

Difficulty: difficult

Hike type: out and back

Trail: packed dirt

Typically open: mid-July - Oct.

Best time of year: Aug. - Sept

Features: forest, alpine meadows, lakes, mountain views

Fees/permits: Northwest Forest Pass required

Agency: Detroit Ranger Station, Willamette National Forest (see pg. 126)

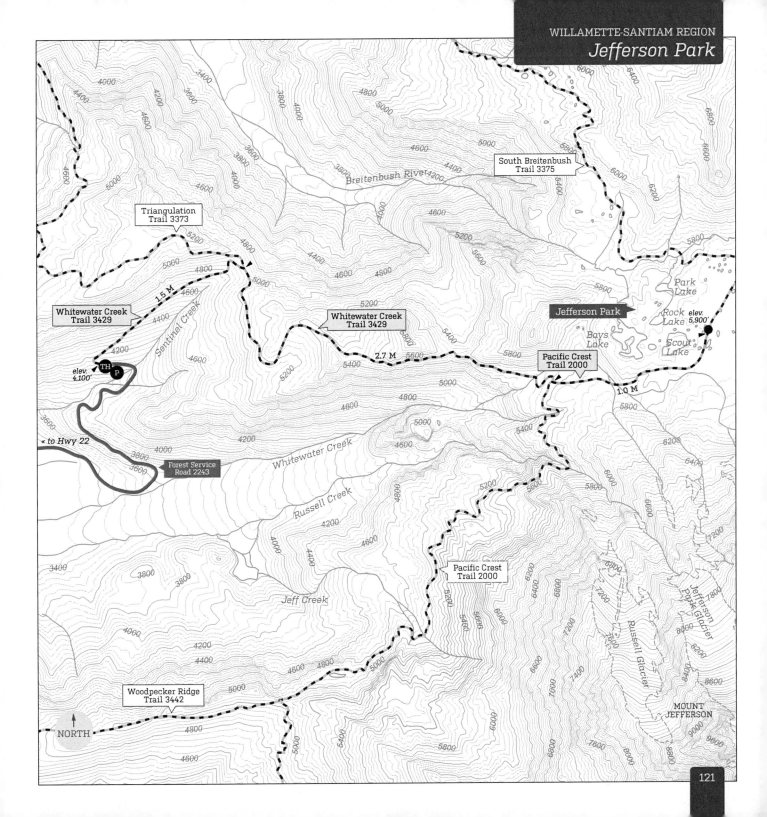

South Breitenbush
Trail 3375

Breitenbush River

Triangulation
Trail 3373

Park
Lake

Jefferson Park

Rock
Lake

elev.
5,900'

Bays
Lake

Scout
Lake

Whitewater Creek
Trail 3429

Whitewater Creek
Trail 3429

1.5 M

2.7 M

Pacific Crest
Trail 2000

1.0 M

Sentinel Creek

elev.
4,100'

TH
P

« to Hwy 22

Forest Service
Road 2243

Whitewater Creek

Russell Creek

Jeff Creek

Pacific Crest
Trail 2000

Jefferson
Park Glacier

Russell Glacier

Woodpecker Ridge
Trail 3442

NORTH

MOUNT
JEFFERSON

Hike through an old-growth forest along the crystal clear Little North Santiam River, with impressive waterfalls and emerald green pools, while glimpsing old mining and sawmill relics along the way.

DIRECTIONS

From Portland, drive south on I-5 to the highway 22 Detroit Lake/Bend Exit 253.

Drive east on highway 22 for 22.5 miles to a flashing yellow traffic light, turning left on the Little North Santiam Road.

In 15 miles, the pavement ends.

Stay on this rough gravel road with plenty of potholes for another 5.6 miles (staying left at two junctions) to the gated trailhead.

Drive time from Portland: about 2 hours

THE HIKE

This is a hike with a lot of Oregon history. The trail begins on a gated gravel road to Jawbone Flats, a former mining town with buildings dating from the late 1920s. The area was originally a summer camp for the native Santiam tribe, where for hundreds of years they met to trade items from the Pacific Northwest. In the 1850s, gold was discovered, and mining for lead, zinc, copper, and silver continued until the 1980s. There was also an operating sawmill, Merten Mill, until the 1940s when it burned down. In the 1980s, there was much controversy over logging the area, and after a twenty-year legal battle, it was designated as a protected scenic wilderness area. Old mining and sawmill machinery and vehicles are scattered throughout the wooded areas alongside the trail and in the tiny town.

The trail traverses the forest next to the Little North Santiam River, with waterfalls and deep pools of emerald green water along stretches of this crystal clear river. The first 2 miles are on the gravel road that residents of Jawbone Flats can drive on, but all hikers park behind the gate at the trailhead. Along this first section of trail, there is an old mining shaft located on the left side of the trail, and several side trails on the right side that lead to viewpoints.

About 2 miles in, a side trail leads to an area filled with old mining and sawmill machinery. Look for an old building that is barely still standing, and the trail beside it that goes towards the river. This leads to impressive Sawmill Falls, the end of the line for the winter run of steelhead coming up this river.

Back on the trail, in another 0.2 miles is a bridge going over the river to the Opal Creek Trail. Both the road and this loop trail lead to Jawbone Flats, so turning right to cross the bridge is a nice alternative to the road trail. The trail traverses the hillside next to the river and crosses several smaller tributaries on rustic bridges before reaching Opal Pool, a deep pool with high walls of rock surrounding it. Just above the pool, the water chutes through a narrow gorge with a bridge above that leads back to the road and Jawbone Flats. From here, take the road all the way back to the trailhead.

Distance: 7.1 miles (roundtrip)

Elevation Gain: 300 ft.

Difficulty: easy to moderate

Hike type: out and back with a loop

Trail: gravel road, packed dirt

Typically open: all year, but snow in the winter prevents access to the loop trail

Best time of year: May - June

Features: mining history, river, creeks, waterfalls

Fees/permits: Northwest Forest Pass required

Agency: Willamette National Forest (see pg. 126)

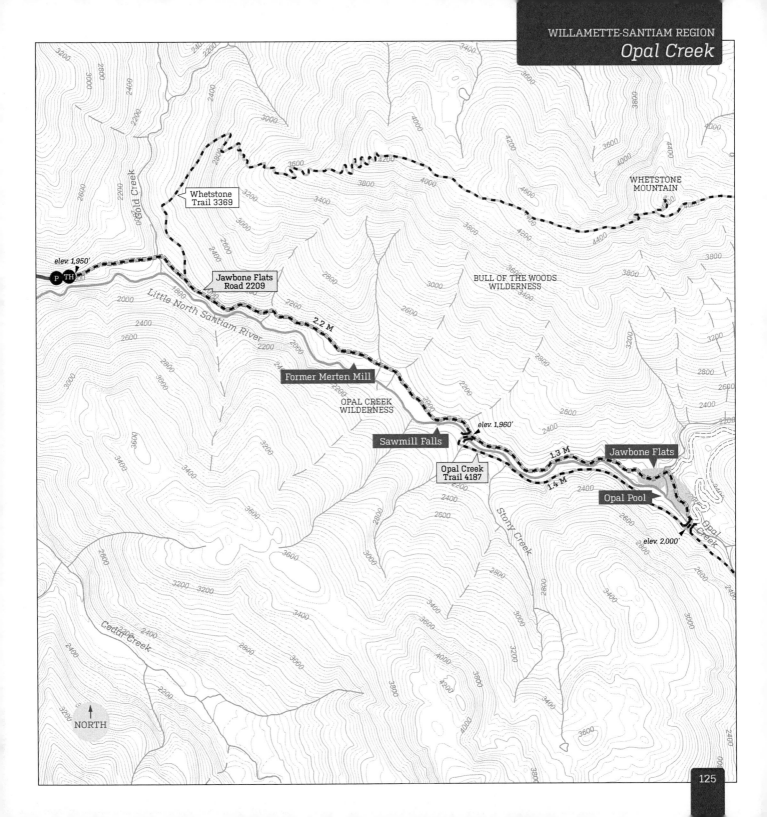

Whetstone
Trail 3369

WHETSTONE
MOUNTAIN

elev. 1,950'

P TH

Jawbone Flats
Road 2209

BULL OF THE WOODS
WILDERNESS

2.2 M

Former Merten Mill

OPAL CREEK
WILDERNESS

Little North Santiam River

Gold Creek

Sawmill Falls

elev. 1,960'

1.3 M

Jawbone Flats

Opal Creek
Trail 4187

1.4 M

Opal Pool

Story Creek

Opal Creek

elev. 2,000'

Cedar Creek

↑
NORTH

Hiking Resources

HIKING INFO

All Trails **alltrails.com**

NW Hiker **nwhiker.com**

Outdoor Project **outdoorproject.com**

Pacific Crest Trail Association **pcta.org**

Portland Hikers **portlandhikers.org**

Washington Trails Association **wta.org**

William Sullivan's Oregon Adventures website
oregonhiking.com

ENVIRONMENTAL ORGANIZATIONS

EarthShare Oregon **earthshare-oregon.org**

Friends of the Columbia Gorge **gorgefriends.org**

Oregon Sierra Club **oregon.sierraclub.org**

Oregon Wild **oregonwild.org**

HIKING GROUPS

Mazamas **mazamas.org**

Oregon Trails Club **trailsclub.org**

Meetup.com Portland Hiking Group
meetup.com/Portland-Hiking-Group

BLOGS

Off the Beaten Trail: 50 Unknown Hikes
offthebeatentrailpdx.com

Paul Gerald's hiking blog **paulgerald.com**

Wy'East Blog **wyeastblog.org**

RECREATION PASSES

Northwest Forest Pass **discovernw.org**

Oregon State Parks Pass **oregonstateparks.org**

Washington State Discover Pass **discoverpass.wa.gov**

STATE/FEDERAL ORGANIZATIONS

Columbia River Gorge National Scenic Area
fs.usda.gov/main/crgnsa

Gifford Pinchot National Forest
fs.usda.gov/main/giffordpinchot

Mount St. Helens National Volcanic Monument
fs.usda.gov/mountsthelens

Mount Hood National Forest **fs.usda.gov/mthood**

Oregon State Parks **oregonstateparks.org**

Washington State Parks **parks.wa.gov**

Willamette National Forest **fs.usda.gov/willamette**

TIDE TABLES

Oregon Coast Tide Tables
or.usharbors.com/oregon-tide-charts

Cannon Beach Tide Tables
cannonbeachlive.com/tide-tables

TOURISM

Oregon Coast Visitor Association
visittheoregoncoast.com

Travel Oregon **traveloregon.com**

Washington State Travel **experiencewa.com**

WEATHER CONDITIONS

Oregon road conditions and webcams **tripcheck.com**

Mountain Forecast **mountain-forecast.com**

National Snow Analyses **nohrsc.noaa.gov/nsa**

WILDFLOWERS

Oregon Wildflowers **oregonwildflowers.org**

Wildflowers of the Pacific Northwest **pnwflowers.com**

Index *(continued)*

Made in the USA
San Bernardino, CA
17 April 2017